The Making of a Television Commercial

H. TED BUSCH & TERRY LANDECK

The Making of a Television Commercial

Macmillan Publishing Co., Inc.

NEW YORK

Collier Macmillan Publishers

LONDON

Macmillan Publishing Co., Inc.
866 Third Avenue, New York, N.Y. 10022
Collier Macmillan Canada, Ltd.

Library of Congress Cataloging in Publication Data
Busch, H Ted.
The making of a television commercial.

1. Television advertising. I. Landeck, Terry, joint author. II. Title.
HF6146.T42B87   659.14'3   80-23192
ISBN 0-02-518830-5

10 9 8 7 6 5 4 3 2 1

Designed by Jack Meserole

Printed in the United States of America

for Dale, Robbie, and Adam
HTB

for Peter, Tim, and Megan
TL

CONTENTS

Contents

PREFACE

Terry's mother wasn't exactly overjoyed when she got into this business: "A nice girl from Kansas should be married, have kids, stay home, and raise a family."

Ted's mother had even more trouble. She thought he should be a dentist or a lawyer or even a salesman. But television commercials! What could she tell the neighbors? "My son makes commercials (whatever that means)?"

Neither of them understand that making commercials is serious business. Both asked time and again, "Well, just exactly what is it that you do?" We dedicate this book to our mothers in the hope that, after reading it, they will know at last just what it is we do.

The Making of a Television Commercial is an overview of the advertising/TV-commercial production world intended to enable the reader—as well as our mothers!—to arrive at an advertising agency or on a commercial film stage and feel comfortable there, because the book will have given him or her a clear understanding of who the people are and what they do. It should be a "head start" for anyone aspiring to join us in any part of this business. The advertising/production industry is challenging, exciting, always changing, difficult, yet rewarding. Each area requires a special talent, long hours, and devotion.

The Making of a Television Commercial

It's a highly competitive field, but one with room at all levels for those who have the creativity and determination.

The book is a tour through the world of television advertising and production. Won't you join us?

ACKNOWLEDGMENTS

We would like to give our thanks to the people listed below for the information, materials, and support they have given us to make this book possible.

Jane Altschuler, Heather Barbash, Julie Begel, Nancy Bennett, Marguerite Birnbaum, Patt Bodene, Judith Broadway, Fletcher Cochran, Bobby Dolan, Lloyd Fink, Lee Fisher, Paul Fisher, Rita Frierson, Byron Gibbs, Jerry Gilman, Judy Goldstein, Jane Haeberly, Tom Herskovits, Steve Hunter, Adam Holender, Dennis Harrington, Ed Kahn, Sally Kandle, Johanna Knowles, Ralph Koch, Don Krakaur, Mardee Kravit, R. Kosoff, Dick Langenback, R. L. Love, Tim Love, Todd MacNichol, Heather Madoff, Philip Mandel, Sheila Manning, Herbert Marks, Mel Matz, John McShane, Michael Millaly, Frank Minerva, Elaine Morris, John Palmer, Suzanne Pancrazi, Jim Phox, Irma Puckett, Stuart Raffel, Bob Ramsey, Ene Riisna, Ellen Ribner, Victoria Rindom, Charlotte Rosenblatt, Lorraine Steurer, Marie Sabat, Peter Scheer, Jack Sidebotham, Les Sunshine, C. Sforza, Ann Terry, Mickey Trennor, Sandy Vogel, Joel Weisman, Joel Weissman, Bob Wilvers, Francine Wilvers, Barbara Wise, Jay Wolf, Oxberry Corporation, Hazeltine Corporation, Magnasync/Moviola Corporation, Shulman Berry Kramer Productions, Inc.

. . . and with special thanks to our editor Toni Lopopolo for her warm encouragement and continual support.

The Making of a Television Commercial

INTRODUCTION

The first thing you notice when you walk onto a sound stage where a commercial is being filmed is the organized chaos. There will usually be as many as twenty people, all going in different directions, each doing something different.

Two men are wrestling with a large lamp (called a "deuce"), trying to get it up ten feet in the air. Another man is on a ladder, holding a long pole with a microphone attached to one end. Over in the corner a man is sitting behind a card table with a tape recorder on it, working hard at what turns out to be the morning newspaper's crossword puzzle.

The set itself looks like a middle-class American kitchen, with two crucial exceptions—a wall is missing and there's no roof. In the set you see two women dressed in slacks and blouses—one with her hair up in curlers, talking to a man in a rumpled shirt and blue jeans. In front of them is a large camera resting on what appears to be a trolley with two swivel seats; this is called a "dolly."

Another man is moving quietly around the set with his light meter, checking the light levels. "Let's hit the table with a deuce," he calls out.

A light is turned on and aimed at the kitchen table. "That's it, now I'm reading a perfect four." (This means that his expos-

1

ure reading for the camera lens is f/4.) He turns to the man in the rumpled shirt.

"We're all set, Steve."

"Thanks, Pete—okay, gang, let's make movies."

Suddenly, all attention is turned to the area in front of the camera. The man with the light meter climbs onto the dolly and sits in position to look through the lens of the camera. Rumpled Shirt stands next to the camera to see the action. A young woman comes up to him.

"We have five seconds for this scene, Steve."

"Right! Everyone set?"

Curlers are removed from the first woman's hair, while someone quickly puts a final touch of lipstick on the other woman. The two women take their positions on the set—one standing by the sink, the other sitting at the table.

A young man moves in front of the camera. He is carrying a small board on which is printed the name of the production company, the name of the commercial, and the number of the scene. This is called a "clapstick" because the top of the board is hinged so that it can be raised and "clapped" down at the beginning of each take. This creates a visible mark on the film, which can be matched to the sound of the clap on the audio tape that is recording the sound. This will be used to synchronize the sound track to the film.

"We're ready, Steve."

"Roll—sound."

The man behind the tape recorder turns it on.

"Speed!"

A button is pushed on the camera.

"Rolling."

The young man with the clapstick calls out, "Sound one." Bang! The stick is clapped.

"Okay, Judy and Chris, we've got five seconds for this scene. Let's not rush it—and action."

The woman by the sink moves to the table with two cups of coffee.

"All set for the party tomorrow night, Helen?"

"Almost, but I could sure use a helping hand cleaning up."

The action stops abruptly with a loud "Cut!" from Steve. "That was fine," he says, "but Judy, you looked a little uncomfortable crossing to the table with the coffee. Let's do another take."

A young woman dressed in blue jeans leaves a group of people who have been standing in the background watching the scene. She walks toward the camera.

"Steve, the client wants Chris to deliver her line with a little more sparkle."

"No problem, she's just warming up—Chris, could you be a little more up this time, a little more like you're trying to con Judy into helping you?"

"Sure, Steve."

"All right, let's do another take."

This scene is typical of what you might find at the filming of a television commercial, which often takes eight to ten hours to shoot. But who are all these people and how did they get here? What are they doing—and why?

In the last thirty years television-commercial production has become an industry, and these people are part of that industry. The very first film television commercial was aired in 1949, and with that airing the industry was born. Since then we have seen more and more sophisticated and creative use of the film medium. In fact, some of the special effects, lighting, and camera techniques seen in motion pictures were first used in television commercials. Also, there have been great strides in the area of electronic photography since the perfection of videotape in the mid 1950s.

Before 1949, anyone wanting to do a television commercial had no choice but to do it live. Today a television commercial can be produced in one of two ways: on film or videotape. Many local advertisers use videotape because it's a relatively fast, easy, and inexpensive way to produce a simple, straightforward advertising message, and most local advertising is fairly simple and straightforward. There is a marked difference in the look of a commercial shot on videotape, however. The action looks live, like it is happening *now*, at the moment it is being seen on television.

Most national commercials are shot on film, however, because film has a softer, more gentle look on television and many advertising agencies believe this quality enhances their advertising. And while it costs about the same to produce a commercial on film or videotape, it costs considerably less to ship film prints of the commercials to stations all around the country because they are much less bulky.

No matter how a commercial is produced, its purpose is the same: to communicate an advertising message. And the purpose of advertising is to inform the general public of a product's performance and/or function, and to stimulate enough interest in it to convince the viewer to buy it.

A great deal has been said about how powerful television advertising can be. Some people think that good persuasive advertising can make viewers buy a product whether or not they want or need it. The fact is that, though good advertising can convince people to try a product once, they won't buy it again if the product doesn't perform as promised, no matter how good or persuasive the advertising. There are many case histories of products with good advertising that disappeared from the market because they didn't deliver what the advertiser promised or the consumers wanted.

As previously pointed out, the function of a television commercial is to communicate an advertising message to the consumer. But that's not an easy job, considering that the average television viewer is exposed to over five hundred commercials

every week.* For one commercial to break through all that
"clutter" and deliver its message is very difficult. Simply stating
that one's company has developed a new detergent or a better
breakfast cereal isn't necessarily going to get the message across.
The challenge is to deliver the message in an interesting and
meaningful manner—and this is where the creative side of advertising comes in.

Assume for a moment that you're the advertising manager of
your own company and you've got to produce a television commercial for your product. The questions you should ask yourself
about any proposed commercial are: Does it say the right things
about the product? Does it point out the important attributes of
the product? Does it communicate how your product is different
or better than your competition? Will the commercial talk in a
meaningful way to the consumers who would use your product?

Once you are sure that the right things are being directed at
the right audience, you have to decide on the best way to deliver your message. There have been many different executional
forms developed to get across such advertising messages, so let's
take a look at some.

SLICE OF LIFE

This is probably the most common format in package-goods
advertising. It usually consists of a little play in which two or
more people are talking about your product—for example, two
housewives discussing the advantages of one dishwashing liquid
over another or a man telling his wife how much he loves or
doesn't love her coffee.

This kind of commercial can be quite effective because it
gives you the opportunity to talk about your product in "people"
terms. Its strength lies in the use of realistic dialogue and in the
dramatization of a situation to show consumers what your prod-

---

* Based on the A. C. Nielsen Co. estimate that the average viewer watches twenty-
six hours of television a week, and the fact that in each hour there are twelve commercial minutes, many of which consist of two 30-second commercials.

uct is, how it works, and what its benefits are. Creating a short scene based on the product can help the viewer see just how it will relate to his or her own life, and what problems, however small, it can solve. When properly done, the slice-of-life commercial can be a strong selling tool which can even include a demonstration of how your product works.

One problem with slice-of-life commercials is that the dialogue spoken by the actors often seems stilted, not the way real people talk at all. Another problem may be that the situation presented is unreal or that there may be too many words for the actors to say comfortably in the short time allowed. When the dialogue isn't real or the situation seems forced, or if the dialogue is rushed to fit into a fixed time, the slice-of-life format can work against you because your playlet won't be believable and the viewers may have trouble following the story.

CONTINUING CHARACTER

In continuing-character commercials the product is presented over a period of time by one actor playing the same character over and over. For example, Mr. Whipple has been cavorting around grocery stores for Charmin tissue for over fifteen years. And for almost that long, too, Madge, the manicurist, has been softening her customers' hands in Palmolive dishwashing liquid. Another example is Rosie, who keeps her diner so tidy with Bounty, "the quicker picker-upper" paper towels. These characters have become totally identified with the products they represent and seem to be authorities on how well they perform.

PRESENTER

The presenter format features a professional performer speaking directly to the viewer. There are two kinds of presenter commercials: the "stand-up" presenter, in which the product spokesman is presented as an announcer speaking to the viewer about your product's virtues; and the "dramatized" presenter, in which an actor or actress plays a character, such as the friendly neighbor or housewife, talking to the viewer.

MUSIC

Music is the star of this type of commercial. A musical theme with special lyrics is created for identification with your product. One example of this format is the Dr. Pepper commercials, featuring people singing that they're peppers "and wouldn't you like to be a pepper too?" The McDonald's commercials sing that they "do it all for you," and convince the viewer that "you deserve a break today." The Bell System has asked the viewers to "reach out and touch someone."

Musical commercials are among the most expensive commercials to produce. Union songwriters, musicians, singers, and dancers are usually acquired at great expense. Moreover, extravagant commercials with large casts and fancy sets require extensive rehearsals and extra time in production to bring all of the pieces together.

VIGNETTE

The vignette format features several short scenes involving different actors or situations, all of which make the same point. A classic use of the vignette format was the Benson & Hedges campaign, which demonstrated, in three different situations, the possible "disadvantages" of their extra-long cigarette. Actually, by this clever use of reverse examples, they were pointing out to the viewers that they were being short-changed by smoking their regular brand of standard-sized cigarettes instead of B&H.

The vignette format works best when there is just one simple point to be made. Its effectiveness results from making the same point several times over, leaving the viewer with a very clear impression of what your product is and what it does.

Vignette commercials can also be expensive to produce. Each scene needs a different set or location and often different actors. This takes time and money; in fact, one vignette commercial with three different scenes could possibly take two days to shoot and cost as much as two simple slice-of-life commercials. Nevertheless, this format can work very well. Both Pepsi Cola and Coke, for example, have had excellent advertising results by using vignettes and adding music.

TESTIMONIAL

The testimonial commercial features actual consumers talking about the virtues of a product. This can be the most convincing kind of advertising because there isn't a copywriter alive who can write dialogue better than that actually spoken by a "real" person.

Testimonial commercials have earned excellent marks for believability. Still, their thrust has been blunted in recent years because of an epidemic of testimonial campaigns. Today the public is tiring of the man next door saying nice things about the wax he uses on his car. The new creative challenge is to develop a situation in which the consumer is actually demonstrating your product in some way, not just sitting there telling the viewer how great he or she thinks it is. This use of testimonial advertising involves the viewer and therefore makes your product that much more desirable.

ANIMATION

Not surprisingly, animation is a very good way to advertise to children. Animation, however, can be quite effective in reaching the adult market too, especially when combined with live action. Starkist Tuna used the "Charlie the Tuna" character successfully for many years, combining the animated antics of Charlie with actual shots of their tuna fish being prepared in many different ways.

Animation can add a little magic or mystery to your product, but of all the different executional formats, animation commercials take the longest time to produce. First, a "character model" of each of your characters has to be created; these are drawings of how your characters should look. Once the character models are created it takes days, sometimes weeks, to draw the many pictures necessary to animate them. After they are drawn, the pictures have to be painted. Then they are photographed in order to create the final animation. Animation can be a lengthy and expensive proposition.

TABLETOP

There are no people in a tabletop commercial, only close-up shots of your product and/or demonstrations of how it works. In a tabletop commercial, your product is the star.

The tabletop format is especially effective for food products. Melted butter rolling down the sides of a freshly baked loaf of bread, a delicious variety of cheese, or a salad dressing being poured onto a delectable, crispy green salad can tickle the taste buds of viewers who aren't even hungry.

Tabletop commercials are a choreography of beautiful and appetizing products. Their success depends on the skill of a tasteful and extremely talented cameraman.

These, then, are the formats that you, as an advertising manager, could choose from. Properly thought out and executed, one or a combination of two or more should result in a commercial that could break through the clutter on television and deliver your advertising message effectively.

Although a commercial is only a thirty- or sixty-second advertising message shown on television, the story of how it gets there is not the least bit simple. It involves a client who has something he wants to sell, an advertising agency that can supply the creative horsepower, and production and editorial companies to deliver the technical expertise necessary to turn an idea on a piece of paper into a fully produced television commercial.

To help tell this story, we have invented a product, Cleen-Up, an all-purpose spray cleaner. Cleen-Up is a product of B & L Consumer Goods Corporation and not only helps clean countertops, walls, and appliances, but can also be mixed with water for cleaning floors.

In *The Making of a Television Commercial*, you will learn about the different job functions in the Advertising/Television Commercial Production Industry. You will also meet people who are composites of the many we interviewed throughout the industry. In our story you will see how these people work together to develop a commercial for Cleen-Up, from its beginnings as an idea to the final advertising that goes on the air.

THE CAST OF CHARACTERS IN

The Making of a Television Commercial

B & L ADVERTISING AGENCY

Sandra
Account Executive

JoAnne
Producer

Ritchie
Writer

Charlie
Art Director

THE CLIENT

Jack
Brand Manager for Cleen-Up

Ann
His Assistant

MS PRODUCTION COMPANY

Steve
Director

Mike
Production Manager

Margaret
Sales Representative

11

The Cast of Characters

THE CREW AND TALENT FOR THE
"HELPING HAND" COMMERCIAL

Lee
Set Designer

Randy
Assistant Director

Pete
Cameraman

Dale
Script Supervisor

Frank
Editor

Tom
Sound Mixer

Judy
Actress ("Mom")

Chris
Actress ("Helen")

Suzy
Child Actress

Adam
Voice-over Announcer

THE CREW AND TALENT FOR THE
HIDDEN-CAMERA TESTIMONIAL

Andy
Director

Rob
Interviewer

Harry
Production Assistant

Mrs. Smith
Shopper

OUTSIDE SERVICE

Sally
Casting Director

AND THE REAL PEOPLE

Lloyd Fink
Associate Creative Director

Paul Fisher
Editor

Suzanne Parcarzi
Editor

Stuart Raffel
Assistant Producer

John McShane
Commercial Director

Elaine Ribner
Advertising Agency Producer

Elaine Morris
Advertising Agency Producer

1. *The Client*

Any discussion about advertising and commercial production has to start with the product and that product's reason for being.

At the turn of the century most companies sold only one product. Ford manufactured only one kind of car; Gillette sold only razor blades; and in Battle Creek, Michigan, Dr. Post and his friend, Mr. Kellogg, were each manufacturing only one brand of cereal: corn flakes. The companies were small and therefore easily run by a few people. It was efficient for these companies to have one management person involved in every level of its product's life. In fact, in some cases, the owner of the company, the president of the company, and the inventor of the product were one and the same man. If there was a problem at the plant, he would go and personally handle it. If his salesman needed some support to make a sale, it wasn't unheard of for him to show up and make the sales pitch himself. He was completely involved in the advertising of his product because he knew, better than anyone, how his product worked and how it would benefit the consumer.

Today, most corporations that sell their products to the consumer have many products in several categories. This is true whether we are talking about General Motors or General Mills.

Gone are the days when it was easy for one man to handle a company successfully, develop the product, and manage the sales and advertising on a day-to-day basis. Now the "product manager," or "brand manager," system of marketing is the one most widely used in America. With this system, corporations set up separate manufacturing, product development, and sales divisions. They also have an advertising division with brand, or product, managers who coordinate the efforts of the others on a product-by-product basis.

Quite simply, a brand manager is the person responsible for the marketing of a certain brand. It is his job to see that the brand grows and stays healthy in the marketplace. In a sense, his position is like that of the president of a small company within a large corporation.

A brand manager has to communicate well, so he must be able to think and speak clearly. Everyone with whom he is involved must understand exactly what he expects of them.

Though verbal communication is important, a brand manager must also be able to communicate in writing. In the world of advertising, everything begins and ends on paper. Even an agreement or arrangement made by telephone ends up in a written report so that there will be no future misunderstanding about any conversation. The report also enables everyone involved with the brand to share the information it contains.

Like the men who ran companies at the turn of the century, the brand manager of today is involved with the total life of his brand. He works with the product-research-and-development people to understand what his product can do and how it can be constantly improved to keep up with the competition. He works with the manufacturing people to understand the process by which his product is made at the plant and with the salespeople who have the responsibility of selling it in the marketplace. He also works closely with an advertising agency which will have the creativity and media expertise to help with the product's advertising.

Because there are so many individuals involved with a

brand, a brand manager must be able to deal capably with people. He should be sensitive and understanding of those he works with, in order to elicit from them their best performances. A good brand manager also inspires a sense of loyalty to the brand, making everyone involved feel an important part of the work team. In a very real sense, a brand manager must be a dynamic, motivating, and involved leader.

The brand manager for Cleen-Up is a gentleman named Jack. He graduated from the University of Michigan with an MBA about six years ago, and immediately joined B & L. Jack worked as an assistant brand manager for two years before being promoted to brand manager on another of B & L's products. He has been brand manager for Cleen-Up for the last year and a half.

Though Jack is head of the Cleen-Up Company, there are managers within the larger corporation to whom he must report. When he is planning an advertising campaign, this is the way the system operates:

Jack collaborates with various groups in the company and at the advertising agency to formulate plans for marketing and advertising Cleen-Up. When they come up with a plan or a piece of advertising on a specific project that Jack thinks will work, he turns his efforts toward convincing his management that the plan is a good one for the product. When he gets their approval to implement it, Jack works to see that all aspects of the plan are properly coordinated.

For the purpose of this story, let's suppose that since its introduction to the consumer several years ago, Cleen-Up has been running only sixty-second TV commercials. These feature a vignette format showing an actress playing a housewife in several different situations. In each situation she demonstrates the product and explains how and why it works.

About two years ago Cleen-Up became the Number Two brand in its category. Recently, however, several new products have come on the market and Cleen-Up's sales have fallen off somewhat, causing concern in the company.

Jack asked the agency to analyze the situation. Was the advertising for Cleen-Up telling the right story? Was there anything they could do in the format to strengthen the product's appeal to the consumer? Should the format for the commercials be changed to tell the Cleen-Up story in a more convincing way?

At the same time, Jack worked with his product-research people to see if the product was the best it could be at this time. Was there any weakness in the product that would prompt consumers to switch to the competition?

The product-research group checked Cleen-Up against its competition. They checked its performance. They checked the formula again. They even interviewed five hundred housewives for their views about liquid cleaners. They then reported to Jack that Cleen-Up was a very good product, with no significant weakness. They also reported that, technically, no competitive product was any better than Cleen-Up.

The report Jack received from the advertising agency indicated the source of the problem. Their analysis showed that while the Cleen-Up commercials were telling the story effectively, too few people were seeing them. The agency recommended that Jack move from all sixty-second commercials to a plan that relied heavily on thirty-second commercials. Since it costs less to buy thirty seconds of time on television, this would allow the airing of more Cleen-Up commercials for the same amount of money and hopefully reach more people with the Cleen-Up story.

Jack agreed the plan was a good one, but was concerned because there weren't any nighttime programs included. He asked Ann, his assistant, to study the media figures sent over by the agency to see if nighttime programs made any sense. Then he asked the agency to create a good thirty-second commercial to go along with the media plan so he could recommend the whole package to his management.

2. *The Agency*

The agency handling the advertising for Cleen-Up occupies several floors in a tall office building in midtown Manhattan. It employs several hundred people and handles about fifteen accounts besides Cleen-Up. The agency and the client act as partners in building a product's image in the consumer's mind, determining its direction in the marketplace, and increasing sales.

An advertising agency is usually made up of several different departments, all designed to service the agency's accounts:

MEDIA

This department consists of media counselors and time-and-space buyers. It works to develop plans for the selection of media by the client. For example, would it be better to communicate the client's message in magazines or on radio or television? How many times should the message appear, and where?

The Media Department also purchases time on radio and television, and space in magazines.

CREATIVE

This is where the writers and art directors "live," where ideas for the client's advertising are born, nurtured, and eventually presented to him* for his approval.

Advertising agencies organize their Creative Departments in one of two ways: (1) with writers and art directors working independently of each other, or (2) with writers and art directors working together as a "team."

In the first instance, a writer is given the assignment to develop a commercial. He works by himself to create a concept and write a script for the commercial. The art director then helps visualize the concept created by the writer by drawing a storyboard (which is like a comic-strip version of the commercial). Under this setup, this is the sole function of the art director; he rarely gets involved in the creation of the original idea.

The team concept is different in that both the writer and art director work together. The team is given the assignment to develop the advertising and they collaborate from the beginning to create the concept and execute the storyboard.

PRODUCTION

The Production Department is made up of producers whose responsibility is to take the approved storyboard and, working closely with the writer and art director, supervise its transformation from a written idea into a finished television commercial. Some agencies, however, don't have production departments or producers. In such case, the writer or art director assumes the role of producer and the responsibility of seeing that a storyboard gets properly produced.

---

* The client, of course, could very well be a woman. We use the masculine pronoun here and sometimes in other places solely to avoid the overuse of such awkward constructions as him/her, he/she, etc.

ACCOUNT MANAGEMENT

This group consists of the account executives, their assistants, and their supervisors. The account executive functions as the main contact between the agency and the client, and is also responsible for the coordination of the work done on behalf of the client by the various agency groups.

As leader on the account within the agency, the account executive has to understand the strengths and weaknesses of his client's product, so he can communicate them clearly to the groups he is working with. His function is very similar to that of the brand manager. The major difference between the two is that the brand manager, on the client side, works with the manufacturing and sales of the product; while the account executive, on the agency side, supervises the development, production, and placement of the advertising.

Basically, advertising is a business of personalities. Like the brand manager, a good account executive must have the ability to lead and get along with people. In many ways he is the "man in the middle," trying to sell the agency's point of view to the client and representing the client's point of view to the agency.

The brand manager on the client side and the account executive on the agency side are like the hubs of two wheels, and the axle that joins them is the client/agency relationship which, when running smoothly, means a good partnership for the advertising of a product.

The account executive working on the Cleen-Up account is a woman named Sandra. She received an MBA from Columbia University and has been at the agency for seven years, the last two working on Cleen-Up.

When Jack asked her to analyze the advertising program for Cleen-Up, Sandra went to the different groups within the agency. She asked the Creative Department to look at the advertising to see if and how it could be improved. She talked with the Media Department about when and where the Cleen-Up commercials were being shown on television.

After studying the situation from several angles, Sandra came to the conclusion that, in order to get the most advantage out of the company's limited media budget, only thirty-second commercials should be used. This would provide more TV air time for the Cleen-Up commercials. She had to be careful, though. Just having more air time isn't always the answer. There is a significant difference between "frequency" (the number of times a commercial is shown) and "reach" (meaning the number of different viewers who see a commercial). Just because a commercial is aired several times doesn't mean that different people see it. In fact, it is very possible that many of the same people would see the same commercial over and over.

The Cleen-Up commercials were shown mainly during the day and, working with her Media Department, Sandra developed a plan for placing the commercials on the air that would allow more people to see the advertising more often during the daytime hours. She presented the plan to Jack; he felt it still wouldn't reach enough people and he suggested, as he and his assistant Ann had discussed, that they look at the possibility of including nighttime programming.

Sandra went back to her media people with this suggestion. Accordingly, they developed a new plan that would add night network to pick up the evening audience.

Jack was enthusiastic about the proposed new schedule until Sandra pointed out that the thirty-second commercial could not have everything in it that the sixty-second one had. She explained, "Cleen-Up's story is fairly complicated. We talk about walls, countertops, appliances, and floors. And we have a demonstration in every scene."

"I know, but all of those are important."

"Jack, we just can't cram that much copy into thirty seconds and have a good piece of advertising. You know yourself that the simpler the story, the better the commercial will be."

"What do you suggest we do?"

"Give up the floor-cleaning sequence. Most of the sales come from people who use Cleen-Up as a spray spot cleaner."

"True, but the product's ability to clean floors is an important part of our franchise, and a point that I feel has to be made."

"I understand, Jack. But something has to go."

"I'll tell you what. Go ahead and assign the copy project to your creatives. Let's see what they can come up with. Maybe they can figure out a way to include all the points."

Sandra agreed to talk with the creative team and give them the go-ahead. The conversation ended with her telling Jack that she expected to have something to show him by the end of the following week.

3. *The Creative Team*

Ritchie and Charlie are a creative team. They have been working together for two years and have worked on the Cleen-Up account for the past six months.

Ritchie, the writer, graduated from Northwestern University with a B.A. in English and had planned to be a teacher. He soon found out that teaching wasn't for him, and thought he'd try the advertising field. He joined a small advertising agency in Chicago, where, as a junior copywriter, he spent three years learning to write good advertising copy. He then decided to try his hand in New York, and was offered a job as senior copywriter at the agency handling the Cleen-Up account. He has been there ever since.

Charlie, his partner, grew up in Brooklyn. He went to the High School of Art and Design and then to New York University. After graduation he took a job in the art "bullpen" at a large advertising agency, where he moved from product to product as he was needed to fill in. These varied experiences earned him more knowledge and a promotion to art director in two years. As Charlie would say, he learned his craft on the job. There was only one problem: Art directors at his agency worked only on print advertising for magazines and drew storyboards for television commercials. They weren't involved at all in developing advertising concepts for television, and that's what Charlie wanted to do. So when he was offered his present job at the agency handling Cleen-Up, he joined Ritchie and they've been working together ever since.

By job definition, the writer in a creative team is supposed to be responsible for the words of a commercial, while the art director deals with the pictures. Most teams work so closely together, however, that their jobs overlap, making for close collaboration in the development of the total concept, words, and pictures. Both must be good conceptual thinkers and, though separate individuals, make one creative whole.

Before a creative team can write persuasive advertising, they have to become familiar with the product they are writing about. To do this, the team takes the product home and gets personal experience from using it. Then they talk with the account executive about past advertising for the product, and what the client would like to see in the future. They next consult with the brand manager and his product-research people to find out technical aspects of how the product works, what its strengths are, and what makes it unique. They also study the product's "copy strategy."

The copy strategy is a document that is written jointly by the client and the advertising agency. It embodies the objectives they want to achieve in any advertising and gives the creative team guidance in writing a commercial. Included in the strategy are statements about the purpose of the product, to whom the advertising should speak, and what the image of the product and the tone of the advertising should be.

Once the creative team fully understands the product and the copy strategy, they are ready to begin writing the advertising. This is the hard part of their business—coming up with the idea, the concept for the commercial. Where does an advertising idea come from? The answer is anywhere and everywhere. There is no secret formula for developing an advertising concept.

Ritchie and Charlie know that Cleen-Up is a good product.

They used it at home and know how it works and why. They also know that their biggest problem isn't just coming up with the concept, but coming up with a concept that will work in thirty seconds.

They have studied the previous Cleen-Up advertising which had been sixty-second vignette commercials. They liked that format, but realized, as had Sandra, the account executive, that they couldn't do as much in thirty seconds as had been done before.

Ritchie: "Okay, where do we start?"

Charlie: "Well, the commercials already on the air look pretty good. The concept is, 'Use Cleen-Up all around the house.' How about sticking with several cleaning situations?"

Ritchie: "There isn't time for more than two or three situations at most."

Charlie: "I know. Let's start with a floor-cleaning situation. The client wants us to keep it in if we can. Let's see how it works."

Ritchie: "Well, you pour Cleen-Up into water to wash floors. We could start out with a lady mopping her floor and have the product sitting next to the bucket."

Charlie: "Right. But where do we go from there?"

Ritchie: "Wait a minute. Since most people buy Cleen-Up to use as a spray cleaner, what would happen if we didn't start with the mopping shot, but did a spray-cleaning sequence with the floor?"

Charlie: "I don't follow you."

Ritchie: "Maybe a little kid tracks mud in and there's only a couple of spots on the floor that need cleaning up."

Charlie: "So Mom sprays the spots and—zap!—the job's done."

Ritchie: "Could work, and that way we keep it a simple spray-cleaning commercial. Let's get something on paper. Give me a hand with this typewriter, will you?"

Charlie: "That's it, Ritchie! You just said it—the 'helping

hand.' Instead of just selling Cleen-Up for cleaning all around the house, how about, 'Cleen-Up, it's like having a helping hand when cleaning around the house.' "

Ritchie: "Great! Let's get to work. If we stick with the 'helping hand,' we could start with a close-up of a kid's dirty hand on a clean wall."

Charlie: "Then we pull back, and there's Mom ready with the product and she cleans the wall in a snap."

Ritchie: "Maybe the kid can say something—ah, I've got it. How's this? We start close on the wall and the camera pulls back to reveal this cute kid looking at his mother and he says, 'Sorry I got the wall dirty, Mommy.' "

Charlie: "I like it, but let's use a little girl, like a tomboy. I think it might be cuter."

Ritchie and Charlie are well on their way to creating the concept.

After the creative team develops a clear idea of the concept, they share it with their supervisor to get his input. They do this to be certain that they are on the right track and that the story makes sense. Once they feel pretty confident about the concept they create a storyboard.

The storyboard, as mentioned in Chapter 2, is laid out like a comic strip. It shows the proposed flow of the concept, placing the words and pictures together for the first time. For the storyboard of a thirty-second commercial, the art director may draw as few as six or as many as fourteen different little pictures, called "frames." (The number of frames depends on how complicated the concept is.) The storyboard also indicates where the creative team plans to make camera moves or use special effects in the finished commercial. In a sense, the storyboard becomes a road map of the commercial. It clearly shows what is supposed to happen, and how the scenes change according to the script. Once the storyboard is drawn and the script written, the creative team is ready to present their commercial.

4. *Presenting the Commercial*

In many ways, advertising is creativity by committee. After the creative team create their concept and put it in storyboard form, they present it to several groups within the agency. Each group makes comments and criticisms, and the creative team's concept usually changes slightly with each presentation.

First, the team makes a formal presentation to their creative management (their copy supervisor and/or the creative director). In looking at the storyboard, creative management wants to make sure that the story is delivered in as creative a way as possible. Is the dialogue natural? Do the pictures and the words in the commercial go together (if cleaning is being *talked* about, is cleaning being *shown?*). Does the commercial seem to flow naturally from beginning to end?

Once they are satisfied that the concept will make a good piece of advertising, creative management arranges for the creative team to present their commercial to the account group, which consists of the account executive, his assistants, and his supervisor. Presenting the advertising to them is a major test for the concept, because if the account group likes it, the creative team will get a chance to present it to the client.

In viewing the advertising, the account group checks to see if it meets all the objectives set for the project. Does the concept deliver a meaningful message in thirty seconds? Is it consistent with the image of the product? And, importantly, is it on strategy—that is, does it fulfill the requirements of the product's copy strategy that was jointly written by the client and agency? The account group can be objective on these points because they haven't been actively involved in creating the advertising.

In this meeting, the account executive plays a very unique role. Because he understands the client's marketing objectives, he can speak for the brand group in analyzing how well the concept will meet those objectives. If the advertising fails in this respect, the account executive can suggest ways of refocusing it to bring it closer to where it should be. On the other hand, if the presentation wins the account executive's approval, he can offer the creative team his insights on how to sell the concept to the client.

Yes, *sell the concept!* Seldom does an agency just send the advertising to the client and get immediate approval to proceed to production. There is a selling process that takes place at a "copy meeting." It is at this meeting that the storyboard becomes a valuable tool.

THE COPY MEETING

If you sat in on a copy meeting, the first thing you'd notice would be the nervous excitement in the room. The agency thinks they have a concept that will meet the brand's objectives, but they don't know how the brand manager will react to it. The brand manager is anxious for good copy that can be produced and put on the air where it will help his business, but he has no idea what to expect from the agency.

The meeting takes place in a long, narrow conference room. There are what appear to be chalk trays all along the walls; these are racks that will hold the storyboards where everyone can see them. A table in the center of the room holds the usual coffee carafes, ashtrays, pencils, and pads.

The tension mounts as the participants arrive. The storyboards are placed in the racks facing the wall so the brand manager won't get an advance peek at them and thus spoil the presentation. Though there is no written rule about this, the brand manager, his assistants, and his supervisor will usually sit on one side of the table, while the agency group sits on the other. It's like two armies, ready for battle, facing each other.

After the opening pleasantries, which do little to ease the tension for the creative team, Sandra, the account executive, starts the meeting by reminding everyone of the reason for being there. She states the agency's understanding of the objectives of the project and usually reads the copy strategy. At this point, the meeting is turned over to the creative team.

Charlie, the art director, begins the presentation by talking about the visuals. He unveils the brightly colored storyboards and, frame by frame, walks the brand manager through the visual flow of the commercial.

"Jack, as you see here, we will open in frame one, very close on a little girl's dirty hand as she takes if off a clean wall. Just as we see her hand coming off the wall, we pull back to reveal her mother standing there with a bottle of Cleen-Up.

"In frame two, Mom sprays the product on the wall and cleans off the handprint left by the little girl.

"Then in frame three, we cut to a product shot and zoom to the label so we can dissolve to several cleaning demonstrations. These demonstrations will be on various surfaces in different places around the house—including, as you requested, the floor.

"Then we dissolve to a scene in the kitchen between the mother and a friend, who has just dropped by for a cup of coffee. At the end of this scene we dissolve to a product shot. And that's the commercial."

Several times the term "dissolve" was used in explaining the visual flow of the storyboard. A dissolve is a special effect that enables one scene to fade into another. It is most commonly used to indicate the passage of time between one scene and another.

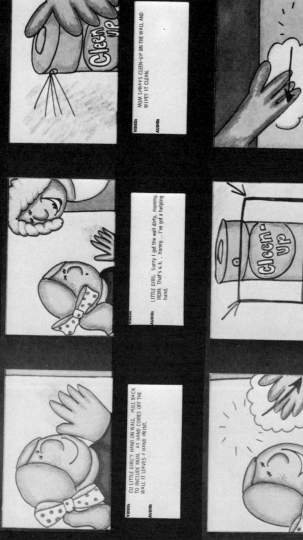

VIDEO: MOM SPRAYS CLEEN-UP ON THE WALL AND WIPES IT CLEAN.

AUDIO:

VIDEO:

AUDIO: LITTLE GIRL: Sorry I got the wall dirty, mommy. MOM: That's o.k. honey... I've got a helping hand.

VIDEO: CU LITTLE GIRL'S HAND ON WALL. PULL BACK TO INCLUDE MOM. AS HAND COMES OFF THE WALL IT LEAVES a HAND PRINT.

AUDIO:

VIDEO: TO VARIOUS CLEANING SHOTS, I.E., COUNTER TOP, FLOORS, ETC.

AUDIO: with those little cleaning chares around the house. Cleen-Up cuts through tough dirt fast and leaves surfaces shining.

VIDEO: PRODUCT SHOT. PUSH IN TO LABEL AND DISSOLVE...

AUDIO: ANNCR VO: That's Cleen-Up! It's like having a helping hand...

VIDEO:

AUDIO: LITTLE GIRL: Wow! That's fast!

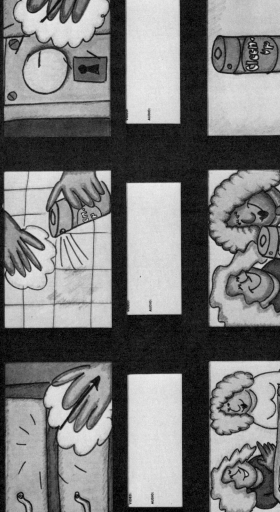

It's like having a helping hand

VIDEO:

AUDIO:

VIDEO: CUT TO PRODUCT SHOT.

AUDIO: ANNCR VO: Cleen-up! It's like having a helping hand to help clean up around the house.

VIDEO:

AUDIO:

VIDEO: MOM HANDS HELEN A BOTTLE OF CLEEN-UP.

AUDIO: MOM: (SMILING) I've got just the thing!

VIDEO:

AUDIO:

VIDEO: DISSOLVE TO LATER THAT DAY. MOM IS HAVING COFFEE WITH A FRIEND.

AUDIO: MOM: All set for the party tomorrow night Helen? Almost...but I could sure use a helping hand cleaning up.
HELEN:

After Charlie finishes his description of the visuals for Jack, Ritchie takes over the presentation to read the copy under the pictures. Actually, he doesn't just read the copy, he acts it out, emphasizing the right words and sometimes even affecting the voice of one or more of the characters if they are important to the concept. Ritchie says:

"As Charlie told you, we open on the little girl's dirty hand and pull back. After the pullback, we see that she is looking at her mother and she says, 'Sorry I got the wall dirty, Mommy.' Mom smiles at her and says, 'That's okay, honey—I've got a helping hand.'

"The little girl watches Mom clean the handprint from the wall and exclaims, 'Wow! That was fast!'

"Then we cut to the cleaning sequences with a voice-over announcer saying, 'That's Cleen-Up! It's like having a helping hand with those little cleaning chores around the house. Cleen-Up cuts through tough dirt fast and leaves surfaces shining.'

"Then we come back to the scene in the kitchen where Mom and her friend Helen are having a cup of coffee. Mom says, 'All set for the party tomorrow night, Helen?' And, Helen, hoping Mom will offer to help clean up for the party, says, 'Almost, but I could sure use a helping hand cleaning up.' Mom smiles and says, 'I've got just the thing.' And she hands Helen her bottle of Cleen-Up.

"Here we cut to the product shot as the announcer reads his line: 'Cleen-Up, it's like having a helping hand to clean around the house.' "

Jack sits in silence. "Will you please read that for me once more, Ritchie?" He picks up a small duplicate of the storyboard from the table and follows the copy as Ritchie reads it again.

When Ritchie is finished reading, Jack spends several minutes studying his copy of the storyboard. These are the longest two or three minutes in advertising. During the time the brand manager is studying the storyboard, every member of the agency team is anxiously awaiting his reaction.

For his part, Jack is trying to absorb the concept, analyze it from several points of view. First and foremost, is it on strategy? Does the concept communicate the main points of the product? Usually this isn't an issue because it has been discussed at great length in the agency long before the copy meeting. Seldom is a storyboard presented that isn't written to the agreed-upon strategy.

The second thing Jack looks for is a persuasive and memorable encapsulation of the strategy, called the "selling idea." The selling idea sums up the concept in a few well-chosen words and is the thought the advertiser wants to leave with the viewers. Often the selling idea is superimposed over a product shot at the end of the commercial. In our case the selling idea is, "Cleen-Up! It's like having a helping hand to clean around the house," so, superimposed over the product shot will be the words: "It's like having a helping hand."

After examining the selling idea, Jack looks for the "key visual." He asks himself if the selling idea is visualized in a memorable way. Since the selling idea for the commercial is "A helping hand to clean around the house," Jack wants to be sure there will be several good cleaning shots. Television is a visual medium, and without the right pictures, a commercial won't sell. In our commercial there are several scenes of Cleen-Up helping to clean off dirt from a variety of surfaces in different parts of the house.

After dissecting the concept, Jack considers the commercial as a whole. Does it flow? Is it realistic? Does it seem to make sense from the consumer's point of view?

The silence is finally broken.

Jack: "I like it. I think it works beautifully. I just have a few comments. I see that you've included a floor visual, Charlie, and I appreciate that; but it's a spray spot-cleaning demonstration rather than a total-floor-cleaning scene."

Charlie: "We took a look at it the other way and it just didn't seem to fit. With just thirty seconds to work with, we felt we absolutely had to simplify the story. Keeping all the cleaning

shots spray shots solved the problem. If we had Mom washing her whole floor, it would take too long to set up and
explain."

Jack: "Can you at least shoot it, and if it doesn't work we won't
use it? What do you think, Ritchie?"

Ritchie: "It's your money, Jack. But setting up that scene will
mean using a larger set and taking more of the shooting day.
In fact, it may mean we'd have to go into a second shooting
day to get that shot for you."

Jack: "How much could it cost?"

Ritchie: "It's hard to say. But it could cost as much as an extra
eight to ten thousand dollars, and in the end I honestly
don't think we could use it."

Jack: "That's expensive. [*He turns to Sandra.*] What do you
think?"

Sandra: "As I told you on the phone, I think most of our usage
is spray spot-cleaning. The boys have done a great job of
getting a variety of visuals in the commercial and I think the
spray visual on the floor will work just fine."

Jack finally bowed to the agency's judgment about the floor
shots, but had some comments for Ritchie about the copy.

Jack: "After Mom wipes the handprint off the wall in frame two,
the little girl mentions how fast it was. Could she also say
something about how clean the wall is?"

Ritchie: "I don't know. We're pretty tight for time."

Jack: "Well, I'd be willing to give up speed for clean if I had to."

Ritchie: "We'll see what we can do."

Jack: "Good. You know, I think the 'helping hand' idea is a
real winner. I just wish there was a way to stress the 'helping' aspect one more time at the end—maybe by repeating
the word 'help' in the announcer's line."

Ritchie: "We'll take a look at that too, okay?"

Jack: "Fine. By the way, how much is all this going to cost
me?"

Ritchie: "We have to bid it out to get an accurate price, but I think we can bring it in for about thirty-five thousand."

Jack: "That's about what we've spent in the past, isn't it, Sandra?"

Sandra: "It's pretty close."

Jack: "All right. When can you get back to me with revisions?"

Sandra: "I expect by the beginning of next week. I don't anticipate any real problems."

The meeting had gone well and everyone was feeling very good about the advertising. When they got back to the agency, Ritchie and Charlie met with Sandra to go over Jack's suggestions. They discussed which ones they felt were valid and which ones they could accommodate.

Jack had made two specific comments about the copy: one about adding the word "clean" to the little girl's line in the beginning; and the other about using "help" in the announcer's line at the end. After looking carefully at the first line, Ritchie and Charlie didn't feel there was time for both "fast" and "clean," so they rewrote the child's line to read, "Wow! That's clean!"

Then they looked at the announcer's line at the end of the commercial. Here they felt they could add the word "help" to have the line read, "Cleen-Up! It's like having a helping hand to help clean up around the house."

In this situation Jack had requested revisions that were relatively minor; but often a brand manager will want changes that are difficult to incorporate into the concept without totally changing it. Sometimes the brand manager will even kill a concept outright if he doesn't think it fits his needs. When this happens, the creative team has to go back and start the process all over again.

In most cases that don't involve drastic changes the agency will either send revised storyboards back to the brand manager or set up another copy meeting to present the revised boards. But not even these steps were necessary in the Cleen-Up situation because the changes were relatively simple and the visuals didn't change. Sandra, therefore, simply sent a revised script to Jack to show him what they had done to incorporate his suggestions. Now the boards read as follows:

Cleen-Up TV :30 Revised "Helping Hand"

1. CU little girl's hand on wall. Pull back to include Mom. As hand comes off the wall it leaves a handprint.

   LITTLE GIRL:
   Sorry I got the wall dirty, Mommy.

   MOM:
   That's okay, honey. I've got a helping hand.

   LITTLE GIRL:
2. Mom sprays Cleen-Up on the wall and wipes it clean.

   Wow! That's clean.

3. Product shot. Push in to label and dissolve to various cleaning shots—countertop, floors, etc.

   ANNOUNCER (VO):
   That's Cleen-Up! It's like having a helping hand with those little cleaning chores around the house. Cleen-Up cuts through tough dirt fast and leaves surfaces shining.

   MOM:
4. Dissolve to later that day. Mom is having coffee with a friend.

   All set for the party tomorrow night, Helen?

   HELEN:
   Almost—but I could sure use a helping hand cleaning up.

   MOM:
5. Mom hands Helen a bottle of Cleen-Up.

   (SMILING) I've got just the thing!

   ANNOUNCER (VO):
6. Cut to product shot.

   Cleen-Up! It's like having a helping hand to help clean up around the house.

5. *Clearing the Commercial*

Once the brand manager is happy with what a commercial says and the way it flows, he begins the process of clearing it through his management and getting their agreement to produce it.

The first step is to make sure that what is said and shown in the advertising is true. It is against the law for advertisers to deceive the public in any way. The claims made in their advertising must be factual and accurate, and any demonstration of the product must be a true depiction of how consumers can expect the product to work in their own homes.

The government agency most concerned with advertising is the Federal Trade Commission. The FTC came into being with the Federal Trade Commission Act of 1914 and is charged primarily with the task of policing "unfair or deceptive acts or practices in commerce." Over the years, the FTC has expanded its charter to include advertising and now keeps close watch over the advertising of any product or service.

To the commission, deceptive advertising means any statement or demonstration which could possibly deceive "the average man on the street." This principle was clearly defined in a case involving the U.S. Retail Credit Association, Inc., which was settled in 1962. In this case the courts ruled that, for a piece of advertising to be ruled illegal, it is not necessary for the FTC to prove that anyone was actually deceived. All they have to prove is that the advertising has a "capacity" to deceive. Thus, anything said in a commercial must be absolutely true. If, for example, a product claims to be the best detergent, the gentlest soap, or the softest tissue, it must be what it claims and have absolute superiority over all its competition. Since it is hard to prove absolute superiority over all competition, however, most advertisers of consumer products are content to make what are called pre-emptive claims, i.e., that they clean well, are gentle to the skin, or are soft to the touch.

The FTC is not only concerned with spoken or written claims of products, however; they are equally interested in visual claims. In the early 1960s, Rapid-Shave Cream was running television advertisements asserting the product had beard softeners and was so moist that even sandpaper could be shaved if it was first softened with Rapid-Shave. This sandpaper-shaving was demonstrated in the commercials—except that sandpaper had not actually been used in shooting the advertising. Instead, the advertiser shaved a piece of plexiglas that had been covered with sand to make it look like sandpaper. The FTC sued the Colgate-Palmolive Company, makers of Rapid-Shave, for deceptive advertising.

This case went all the way to the Supreme Court where Chief Justice Earl Warren rendered a precedent-setting decision that, for the first time, established firm guidelines for television demonstrations:

1. *No television demonstration may use any mock-up, model, or any material which pretends to be something else, without disclosing this fact to the audience.*

In other words, if you claim to be shaving sandpaper, you must be shaving sandpaper or disclose the fact that you aren't.

2. *Any visual or demonstration of a product must be absolutely accurate and truthful.*

For example, in a commercial for vegetable soup, the Campbell Soup Company put marbles in a bowl of soup so that the vegetables would be pushed to the top and show better on television. The FTC charged that this was illegal because the fact that marbles were used to enhance the soup wasn't disclosed in the advertising.

In simple terms, the guidelines mean that anything a consumer sees in a television commercial must be what he thinks it is. For example, if a laundry demonstration shows a dirty shirt being put into a washing machine, it must be that same shirt that emerges clean, and not an identical one that was never dirty. Also, the shirt must be stained with the type of dirt that the viewer believes it is soiled with; it can't be stained with mud if the advertising claims it is stained with grease.

Most national advertisers today are very responsive to their consumers and to the spirit of the law. As we have said, advertising can only convince people to try a product, and if it doesn't perform as expected, they won't buy it again. National products only survive if consumers buy them time and time again, so it is in the advertisers' best interest to make sure that they don't oversell their products, but rather, communicate to the consumer a true representation of them.

In our story, the Cleen-Up commercial claims to clean stains and dirt off a variety of surfaces. Since it actually works the way the advertising says it will, the commercial copy is legal. To make sure that the visuals in the cleaning demonstrations are also legal, Jack asks one of his product-research technicians to be on the set to prepare the dirt that will be used on the surfaces. The handprint on the wall will be mud; the dirt around the stove, bacon grease; and a soap scum will be used around the sink in the shot of the bathroom vanity top.

Now that Jack has determined that the advertising claims are legal and that the demonstrations will be shot accordingly, he is ready to take the next step in clearing the advertising: getting his management's approval to produce the commercial.

Jack: "Sir, as you know we have been getting some pretty stiff competition and over the past six months have seen Cleen-Up's share of the market slip a little."

Manager: "Why do you think that is, Jack?"

Jack: "There have been two new products introduced and we feel that consumers are giving them a try."

Manager: "Do you see this as a serious problem?"

Jack: "No, sir. The agency has developed a plan that will help us hold our share and begin to build again in the next six months. After analyzing the situation, we feel part of the problem is that not enough people are hearing our story."

Manager: "You're currently using sixty-second commercials, aren't you?"

Jack: "Yes, sir, but we are recommending a thirty-second plan that will allow us to get to more consumers with our story more often and stay within our current budget. To implement this plan we are recommending production of a thirty-second commercial called 'Helping Hand.' "

Manager: "You realize, of course, that you can't say as much in thirty seconds."

Jack: "Yes, sir. But this commercial incorporates a new strong selling idea: 'Cleen-Up! It's like having a helping hand to help clean around the house,' and also has a variety of good cleaning visuals."

Jack's presentation is convincing. Management—after reviewing Cleen-Up's marketing situation and the "Helping Hand" commercial—gives Jack the go-ahead to proceed with production.

6. The Producer

Upon receiving the client's approval to proceed, the agency begins the process of turning their concept for a commercial from a piece of paper into a finished piece of advertising. At this stage, a new member joins the agency team—the producer.

The producer is trained to look at a storyboard and decide how to translate it into moving pictures. He is a technical expert in the field of commercial-making; he knows the equipment and how to use it to achieve the desired effects.

Involved as he is in production, the producer is concerned with the look and feel of the advertising and in making sure that everything works from a production point of view. On the other hand, he understands advertising, and works within the production context to see to it that the message of the advertising is communicated clearly. A producer is creative, with a sense of style, a good ear for dialogue, and an ability to understand concepts. But, most importantly, the producer must be able to work well with the agency's writer and art director.

A producer is a problem-solver and the first problem he must solve is that of being an interloper. The creative team has worked weeks, often months, on a concept to get it approved by the client. Then in comes a producer who, until now, has had no exposure to the idea. The challenge facing him is to be accepted as part of the team and to help them turn the concept into a good piece of advertising. Needless to say, he must handle this situation with a great deal of tact.

Objectivity is one of the contributions the producer makes to the creative team. Simply because he hasn't had any prior exposure to their concept, he can approach it from a different perspective. Often a copy project will go back and forth between the client and the agency for several weeks, and by the time production approval is granted, the creative team may have lost much of their objectivity. For this reason a producer's fresh point of view can be a real plus.

The producer assigned to the Cleen-Up project is a woman named JoAnne. She graduated from Michigan State University with a degree in radio and television and, after several years of on-the-job training, has become one of the agency's strongest producers.

When JoAnne is assigned to a project, she immediately meets with the creative team to discuss the concept, for it is important that she become completely familiar and comfortable with the material she is about to produce. JoAnne and the team discuss the kind of location that is needed for the action, the kind of people involved in the story, their background and the clothes they are wearing; they even discuss what time of the year the action is supposed to be taking place. A clear understanding of all the minute details is absolutely necessary if JoAnne is to become a fully active member of the creative/production team.

After her meeting with the creative team, JoAnne returns to her office and times the storyboard. In the world of television advertising you are ruled by the clock. You must submit to the "tyranny" imposed by thirty seconds and it is the producer's responsibility to ensure that the commercial actually works within that time limit.

To determine if this is possible, JoAnne must time the action as well as the dialogue. With a stopwatch, she acts out the commercial. How much time does it take to clean a handprint off the wall? How long does it take Mom to walk to the table with a cup of coffee? Is there time for all the scenes to be natural and relaxed, or will the action have to move too fast to be believable?

There are some concepts that are just too complicated to work out in thirty seconds. Storyboards are overwritten because some agency people and clients want to squeeze into thirty seconds everything they have to say in a sixty-second commercial. This is where the producer's objectivity is most important. She can look at a storyboard with unprejudiced eyes and tell whether it is trying to cover too much or whether there is too much going on visually.

If there is a timing problem, the producer goes back to the creative team and they work together to find a solution, because if a commercial is too rushed, either in copy or visually, there is little chance that it will communicate its advertising message. If that happens, it is a waste of money to produce and air it.

After timing the Cleen-Up storyboard, JoAnne found that the only problem was with the cleaning scenes in the middle:

JoAnne: "We can do one cleaning shot, but there just isn't time to do three or four effectively."

Ritchie: "Why should the cleaning scenes take so long? The product works and it's just a quick wipe."

JoAnne: "Have you timed how long it takes to clean a spot off a wall with the product?"

Ritchie: "No."

JoAnne: "Okay, then, let's start with the basics. What do we need in each cleaning shot?"

Ritchie: "You've got to see the dirt, then the spray, and then the wipe. That's it."

JoAnne: "What about the surface after you've wiped it. Isn't it important to see it clean?"

Ritchie: "Of course."

JoAnne: "Right. Now, let's get out the watch and time that action—Charlie, when I say go, you do it, okay?"

It takes Charlie two seconds to spray and wipe the wall. But that doesn't allow time for the viewer to see the cleaned surface. It is now clearly obvious that four separate cleaning demonstrations cannot be used, so JoAnne suggests using a split-screen effect.

JoAnne: "We could split the screen into four segments and show a different cleaning sequence in each one."
Charlie: "So we'd have four cleaning scenes on the screen at the same time?"
JoAnne: "Right."
Charlie: "I think it will work and that way we will still get good cleaning registration."
Ritchie: "If we do the split screen, will we have any problem bringing the commercial in on time, JoAnne?"
JoAnne: "None at all."
Ritchie: "Then let's do it."

Once they are sure the commercial works in thirty seconds, the team begins the task of selecting a director. JoAnne contacts a number of film production companies and asks them to send their director's sample reel (explained in more detail on page 48). It is from screening these reels that the creative/production team begins to narrow the search for the right director.

What the team looks for when they screen a sample reel is overall quality. How does the director handle the talent? What type of lighting does he use? How does he move the camera? What is the quality of his sets?

According to the Fall 1979 *Motion Picture TV & Theatre Directory*, there are over three hundred commercial directors in New York alone, so the task of selecting the right one isn't easy. One of the producer's responsibilities, however, is to be aware of what directional talent is available, what type of work they are doing, and what the production company backup is. A good director still needs good production assistance to help him execute his creative ideas.

The Cleen-Up team narrows its search to three directors and

they are ready to begin the bidding process in which represen-
tatives of the three directors will be asked to analyze the storyboard to determine the cost of production. In most cases the
production company with the lowest bid will get the job.

7. *The Production Company*

A director, a sales representative, a production manager, and a good line of credit at the bank are the essential ingredients for forming a commercial production company.

The facility to house a production company can be as small or as large as the pocketbook can afford. However, keeping the overhead down helps keep the bank balance up. A number of production companies have started out in the director's home and expanded to larger quarters only after a need for more space became imperative.

For our story we've created MS Productions, which opened its doors in a two-room office in midtown Manhattan. Steve the director, Margaret the sales representative, and Mike the production manager share the front office. The back room is used for accounting, film reels, supplies, and storage. After deciding to go into business, the first thing MS Productions had to do was establish a line of credit with the bank.

GOOD CREDIT

A good line of credit is important because producing a television commercial is expensive. Production costs average a minimum of $10,000 for a single day of shooting, and the production company is responsible for much of this cost up front. The

46

advertising agency will give only one-half of the cost of production to the production company in advance; the rest is paid after the commercial has been edited. Often that can be ninety days after the commercial has been shot.

The production company is responsible for contracting a set designer to design the set and for renting the stage where the set will be built. Then the production company must hire the "crew," the people necessary to build the set and operate the equipment on the day of the shoot. Also, very few production companies own their own equipment because of the expense involved in the purchase, upkeep, and storage. Instead, they rent the cameras, lenses, lights, and other equipment they need on a job-by-job basis. This is a huge expense that is initially borne by the production company.

As a result of all of this, a large flow of cash is an absolute requirement for a production company to stay in business. A moderately busy company might shoot five commercials a month. In a period of ninety days they may have spent as much as $150,000 and yet have received only $75,000. This can put a serious strain on cash reserves. The balance between spending and collecting is always an urgent issue and this is why it is most important for a production company to have a good line of credit at the bank.

THE DIRECTOR

The director is the focal point of the production company. He sets the tone of the company, and much of the company's success rests on his shoulders. He takes the agency's concept and, with his knowledge, background, and talent, turns it into a viewable piece of advertising.

The director is the captain of the production team that is hired to take a concept from a storyboard to a piece of film. He oversees and coordinates all aspects of production. He works closely with the set designer to see that the commercial has the proper environment in which to play, and with the actors to get the right performances. He designs the way the camera shoots the scenes and works with the cameraman to see that the lighting creates the right mood.

Steve, the director for MS Productions, has been directing television commercials for fourteen years. He started out in the industry as an art director, right out of college. He continued working on the agency side of the business for many years, and was a senior art director at one of New York's large advertising agencies when he left to try his hand at directing.

Steve's first contact with the advertising is when his company is asked to bid on a job. The agency gives him a copy of the storyboard, which he goes over carefully, checking to see what kind of set they will need for the commercial and what special equipment might be necessary. Then he analyzes the storyboard to see how many hours he thinks it will take to shoot it. After his analysis, Steve meets with his production manager and sales representative to discuss the job and prepare a bid for the agency.

Once a job has been awarded, Steve meets with the agency team as soon as possible. He wants to get their point of view and understand exactly how they see the commercial developing. All he has been given is a piece of paper with pictures and words on it, and it is his job to bring that paper to life in a clear and artistic way.

THE SALES REPRESENTATIVE

The sales representative is one of the major forces contributing to the success of a director. He introduces and sells the work of his director to the creative/production team at the agency, and this is a tough business because there are so many good companies all competing for the same work.

To help sell his director, the sales "rep" puts together a sample reel, of approximately ten to fifteen of the director's past commercials, chosen as the best representations of the director's style and ability. This reel is one of the most important tools the sales rep has. With it he can help create an image for his director by illustrating the kind of commercials he does well.

Putting together the director's sample reel is one of the easier parts of the job; the most difficult part for the rep is getting to meet with agency creative teams and producers to show them what he's got. The reason for the difficulty is that the agency people may have several different projects going at the same time and they are bombarded every day by production companies wanting to screen their reels for them. What it takes is perseverance: trying to get to know the creative/production teams as people and gaining their trust. It may take months but if the rep doesn't give up he may eventually have a chance to screen his director's reel.

Though screening the sample reel is important in order to show the agency team what a director can do, the matter of personality is also part of the business of creating commercials. Therefore, if the agency team likes the reel, the next step is to have them actually meet with the director, perhaps at lunch. If the creative team and producer are comfortable with a director and satisfied that he will do a good job on their commercial, they may ask him to bid on their next job.

Margaret is the sales rep for MS Productions. When she graduated from New York University, she took a job as receptionist and Gal Friday for a small production company. Because of its size, she was asked to help out in all production areas, and learned quite a bit about making commercials. What she was enthusiastic about, though, was meeting and working with people. She gradually developed an expertise in sales, and when Steve and Mike opened up their company, Margaret joined them as their sales representative, or "sales rep"—which is the term used in the industry.

Margaret tried for months to get the Cleen-Up creative team to screen Steve's reel. Finally, JoAnne, the agency producer, had time to screen with her. JoAnne was delighted with what she saw of Steve's work and when the Cleen-Up job came through, she recommended that Ritchie and Charlie take a look at the reel. They did, and agreed that they should bid Steve for the job.

Margaret, along with reps from two other production companies, was invited to a specification meeting. At a meeting of this kind the producer discusses the commercial in detail and explains what the creative/production team has in mind for sets and props. Other subjects covered are whether the team wants to shoot the commercial on film or videotape, what kind of mood they want to create, and any special shots or effects they want to achieve. When the meeting is over, the production companies' reps have all the information necessary to estimate the cost of the job.

THE PRODUCTION MANAGER

The production manager is sometimes called the "production company producer" because he estimates the cost of shooting the commercial with the help of the director and sales representative, then does his utmost to see that "the shoot" comes in on budget. Putting together a commercial shoot is like putting together a giant jigsaw puzzle, and the production manager makes all the pieces fit. He finds the right set designer, hires the crew, and rents the stage and equipment. Then he arranges to have the crew, the actors, and the equipment all get to the right place at the right time.

Mike, Steve's production manager, graduated from the University of Miami with a business degree and came to New York to find a job. All he could find was a job in a commercial production company as a "go-fer"—the kid who runs all the errands ("Go for this, go for that," etc.). But he found the production business fascinating and spent as much time as he could on the set watching and asking questions, and eventually became a production assistant, a job he held for five years before becoming a production manager. He worked in this capacity for two years and then joined Steve to open MS Productions.

As production manager, Mike keeps track of all the costs of

shooting the commercials. He stays up to date on the constantly changing prices of rental equipment and has learned to make deals with the equipment rental houses to help keep the cost of production down. Mike is also responsible for hiring and overseeing the crew and knows the latest union regulations covering each member.

Simply put, the production manager helps create a budget for a commercial shoot and does everything he can to make sure that the job comes in on budget.

THE PRODUCTION COMPANY MEETING

When Margaret returns to the production company from the specification meeting, she meets with the director and the production manager to discuss the storyboard.

Margaret: "Steve, this is a pretty good commercial for Cleen-Up. It's got two scenes with dialogue and a voice-over middle section with some cleaning demonstrations."

Steve [*looking over the storyboard*]: "The closing scene takes place in the kitchen. Can we shoot the opening scene in the kitchen too?"

Margaret: "No. The agency wants to show that Cleen-Up works all around the house. JoAnne suggested that the opening scene might be a den or a playroom."

Mike: "Could it be a hall?"

Margaret: "She didn't mention that, but I don't see why not."

Mike: "That would be easier to control and cost less to build because we'd only need one wall. What do you think, Steve?"

Steve: "That would work. I'm sure we're going to want to be pretty close to the wall, anyway, to see the stain and the cleaning action."

Margaret: "Speaking of cleaning—JoAnne said that they want one of the cleaning shots to be on a bathroom vanity top."

Mike: "What about the other three?"

Margaret: "One should be an appliance—either a stovetop or a refrigerator. Then they want a kitchen countertop and a floor."

Mike: "Looking at the action, Steve, how big a kitchen set do you think we need?"

Steve: "Well, I think we need at least three walls. We can pick up the kitchen-cleaning shots using the set pieces."

Margaret: "JoAnne said that they were looking for a modern but warm kitchen."

Steve: "Right. That means a built-in oven, dishwasher, a countertop stove, with nice cozy colors and friendly touches around the set."

Mike: "What about the dirt for the demonstrations?"

Margaret: "JoAnne said that the client would have a man from their products-development department come to the shoot and make the stains for the demos."

Next, the matter of camera setups is discussed. A camera setup is the placing of the camera and lights in a set position to shoot all or part of a scene. When the camera must be relocated and the lights changed to continue the scene or begin a new one, it is considered a new setup, and each is a measure of time in production because it usually takes between thirty minutes to an hour to change from one to another. To shoot the Cleen-Up commercial, Steve figures he will need at least seven setups: one for the opening scene between Mom and the little girl; one for the scene between Mom and Helen; one for the product shots in the middle and the end of the commercial; and four for the cleaning demonstrations. Also, because the little girl has dialogue, which will take time, as will lighting the demos, he feels they should plan on a ten-hour-day for shooting. He recommends Pete as the cameraman to get, if he's available, for Pete is good with lights and is a fast worker.

With this information Mike can estimate how much it will cost the production company to produce the commercial. Now he must prepare a bid and submit it to the agency.

8. *Bidding the Commercial*

In the commercial-production industry there are two ways to bid a commercial: firm bid; and cost, plus fixed fee. Before a job is bid, the agency and the production companies agree on which method will be used.

FIRM BID

With the firm-bid method of bidding, the production company is responsible for all costs and overages. The company prepares an estimate and submits to the agency the price they will charge to produce the commercial. Once the figure is agreed upon, it becomes a contract price that cannot be changed. This means that if the job comes in underbudget, the production company keeps the difference between the estimate and the actual cost of the production; if it comes in overbudget, the company must pay the difference.

There are many things beyond the production company's control that could cause a job to go overbudget. For example, an actor might freeze on the set and not remember his or her lines; or the creative group could be undecided on the set about some phase of handling the commercial. Either of these circumstances could cause the shooting day to run longer than planned and use more film than was budgeted. Also, a piece of equipment might malfunction or the agency might require something at the last minute that wasn't accounted for in the budget. To protect themselves against going overbudget because of such unexpected delays or expenses, a production company usually inflates a firm bid beyond what they estimate it will actually cost them to shoot the commercial.

COST, PLUS FIXED FEE

With the cost-plus method of bidding, the production company estimates every cost that they feel will be needed to produce the commercial and submits them to the agency for approval. To these costs the production company adds the director's fee and their "fixed fee," which covers their markup and overhead. Once the job is awarded, any costs over and above what was estimated are paid to the production company, but the fixed fee remains the same. With the cost-plus method the production company doesn't need to inflate the bid to protect themselves; they know they will be reimbursed for any legitimate overages that might occur.

For the Cleen-Up commercial the agency and production companies agreed to use the cost-plus-fixed-fee method of bidding. Therefore, the production manager works with a bid form that lists all the categories involved in preparing and shooting the commercial and helps him figure his "direct costs": what it will cost the production company to do the job. With the addition of the director's fee and the fixed fee, the total becomes the bid that he sends to the advertising agency.

Before we can discuss the bidding of the Cleen-Up commercial in detail, it will be necessary to describe the various crew positions listed on the bid form.

Assistant Director   The director's right hand on the day of the shoot. The assistant director supervises the crew and tries to protect the director from as much pressure as possible. He is familiar with every aspect of the shoot and is empowered to discuss extra budget items or needs with the client.

Cameraman (Director of Photography) Works with the director to help select the best shots for the commercial. The cameraman has the ultimate responsibility for lighting the set and operating the camera.

Assistant Cameraman Responsible for maintaining the camera at the shoot—that is, keeping the wheels and the head that supports the camera oiled, and the batteries on charge. The assistant cameraman loads the film into magazines for shooting and, while the camera is running, makes sure that what is being shot is in focus. He also keeps a record of everything that is shot, recording the amount of footage used and any technical comments about what was shot. He then packs and labels the exposed film and arranges for it to be sent to the lab for developing.

Outside Prop Employed to work before the shoot day, the outside propman gathers the items needed to dress the set or location. On the day of the shoot he may become the inside propman.

Inside Prop Works with the set designer on the day of the shoot. The inside propman places the props in the set and, if necessary, works with the product to prepare demonstrations.

Gaffer (Electrician) Works hand in hand with the cameraman to light the shots. The gaffer takes light-meter readings to be certain the lighting is accurate and, to check its degree of contrast, will often use a Polaroid.

Grip Does all the heavy lifting and moving during the shooting day. The grip moves the dolly on which the camera is mounted, and lifts and moves various set elements to wherever the director wants them. The grip will also set "cutters" and "flags"—pieces of cardboard or black fabric that help control glare from the lights.

Mixer Operates the tape recorder that records the sound track for the commercial. With the aid of very sophisticated microphones and a mixing machine, the mixer avoids unwanted background sounds and extraneous noise, and concentrates on the level and quality of the sound necessary for the shoot. The mixer also keeps a record of everything recorded, which should match the assistant cameraman's record on what is shot. These two records are valuable tools for the editor when it comes time for him to edit the film into a commercial.

Boom Man   Works with the mixer. The boom man handles the "boom," a long pole with a microphone attached to the end. He must reach into the scene with the boom and follow the sound without letting the microphone be seen in the picture.

Makeup Person   Applies the actors' makeup for the shoot. During the day he will be standing by on the set to see that the makeup remains exactly as it was at the beginning of the shoot day.

Hair Stylist   Creates the hairstyles required for the talent on the commercial. The hair stylist also stands by on the set during the shoot to see that all hairstyles remain consistent during the day.

Stylist   Shops for the actors' clothing for the commercial. The stylist is given specifics supplied by the creative team and the director, and will most often select several outfits. The final selection of wardrobe is made by the agency and director. If the actors are requested to wear their own clothing, the stylist meets with them to choose the most appropriate items.

Wardrobe Attendant   Keeps the talents' clothing pressed and repaired during the shooting day.

Script Clerk (Script Supervisor)   Works closely with the director to make certain that no shots are forgotten during the day. The script supervisor is responsible for the continuity and matching of the scenes. For example, if the waitress in a scene has a pencil behind her left ear in scene 1, the script supervisor is careful to see that it's behind the same ear in scene 2. The script supervisor times each scene as it is shot to be sure that when the day is finished the total time of all the scenes adds up to the required time for the commercial. She also keeps "script notes," which include the time of each scene and any comments made about it. These notes, along with the reports from the assistant cameraman and the mixer, go to the editor to serve as aids in the editing process.

Production Assistant   The go-fer for the production company. Before the shoot day, the production assistant might be given the task of picking up small props or other material needed for the job. During the shoot, he stands by to run any last-minute errands.

Teamsters   Drive equipment trucks and cars and help with any necessary loading and unloading. It is a union requirement that teamsters be hired any time a vehicle is used in a commercial shoot, whether on camera as part of the commercial or for transporting personnel or equipment.

Set Designer   Works with the creative team's concept and the director's recommendations to design the set for the commercial. The set designer employs and supervises the painters and carpenters who execute his set design.

One or more of each of these crew members will be hired for every commercial shoot, with the average commercial using at least a fifteen-member crew.

PREPARING THE BID

When Mike sits down with the bid form (see p. 58) to prepare a bid for the Cleen-Up commercial, the first thing he figures out is how much time he needs from each crew member. A normal union shooting day is eight hours, but in discussing this job with Steve, it was agreed that it will take longer than eight hours to shoot. Analyzing the storyboard, Steve feels he will need three and a half hours to shoot the first scene with the little girl; from experience, he knows that it can take a lot of time to shoot a scene where children have dialogue. Then he figures he will need three and a half hours to shoot the cleaning demonstrations, and another three hours—most of which will

A: PRE-PROD'N / WRAP   B: SHOOTING

CREW	ESTIMATED				(Actual)			ESTIMATED				(Actual)		
	Days	Rate	O/T Hrs	Total	Days	Rate	Total	Days	Rate	O/T Hrs	Total	Days	Rate	Total
1. Producer:														
2. Asst. Director:	1	275		275				1			275			
3. Dir. Photography:								1	400	200	600			
4. Camera Operator:														
5. Asst. Cameraman:								1	150		150			
6. Outside Props:														
7. Inside Props:								1	135	68	203			
a.								1	125	62	187			
b.														
c.														
d.														
e.														
8. Electricians:								1	135	68	203			
a.								1	125	62	187			
b.														
c.														
d.														
e.														
9. Grips:								1	135		135			
a.								1	125		125			
b.														
c.														
d.														
e.														
10. Mixer (or Playback:)								1	150		150			
11. Recordist:														
12. Boom Man:								1	125		125			
13. Make-Up:								1	125		125			
14. Hair:								1	125		125			
15. Stylist:	1	200		200				1	75		75			
16. Wardrobe Attendant:								1	125	62	187			
17. Script Clerk:														
18. Home Economist:														
19. Scenics:														
20. VTR Man:														
21. EFX Man:														
22. Nurse:														
23. Telepr. & Operator:														
24. Generator Man:														
25. Still Man:														
26. Loc. Contact/Scout:														
27. P. A.	2	75		150				1	75		75			
28. 2nd A. D.														
29. Teamsters														
a)														
b)														
c)														
30.														
	SUB TOTAL A			625				SUB TOTAL B			2927			

Job Description / Schedule Breakdown

involve lighting and rehearsal—for the last scene between Mom and her friend. In all, they will bid a ten-hour day, which means that Mike will have to figure two hours of overtime for many of his crew members.

The first section of the bid form deals with the crew. It covers pre-production and wrap (the time prior to and following the shooting day) and the shooting day itself. Starting with the first category in the crew section, Mike pencils in one day of pre-production and one day of shoot for an assistant director; the pre-production day will be used to familiarize the assistant director with all the details and logistics of the shoot and fulfill a union requirement that an assistant director must be brought into a production at least one day prior to the actual shooting. Also by union agreement, an assistant director gets the same pay whether he works eight or fifteen hours. Since the Cleen-Up job is budgeted for ten, the assistant director gets only his day rate and no overtime.

The director of photography, or cameraman, is put in for one day of shooting, plus two hours of overtime. Even though it's not required, a cameraman often volunteers to come to the stage the day before the shoot to meet with the director and discuss the shots and kind of lighting he has in mind.

Next comes the assistant cameraman. Mike puts him down for two and a half hours of overtime, a half hour more than the rest of the crew. This is because the assistant cameraman is responsible for taking care of the film and camera after the shoot has been completed.

Mike sees no need to bring in a union propman to collect the few props that might be called for before the shoot. Instead, for two pre-production days and the day of the shoot, he adds a production assistant, who works at a much lower day rate and will be able to get the few articles necessary for the set. The P.A. will help with odd jobs on the day of the shoot, in addition to running last-minute errands.

While no union propmen are necessary before the shoot, Mike figures he will need two inside propmen the day of the shoot. One will put the props in place on the set and the other will work with the client's technician, preparing the dirt for the cleaning demonstrations.

Mike estimates that he will need two electricians (gaffers) for the Cleen-Up job. He determined this by the size of the set they will need and the size and number of lights he feels will be necessary to light the actors and the set area.

Two grips will be necessary. One will push the camera dolly, the other will lift and move various set elements. Grips will also set cutters and flags.

In the Cleen-Up commercial the actors speak during their scenes, so Mike pencils in a two-man sound crew—a mixer to run the tape recorder and a boom man to work with the microphones. Steve is planning to shoot the scenes with dialogue first; therefore the sound crew won't get any overtime because they will be released before the regular eight-hour day is over.

The makeup person and hair stylist will also be needed for a straight eight-hour day, the same amount of time the actors will be on the set.

Since there are no special costumes and the actors are expected to wear their own clothes, Mike puts a stylist in for only one pre-production day. The stylist will review the clothes the actors own and decide if they are appropriate for the commercial. If anything is needed to complete the wardrobe, the stylist will have time to shop for it the same day. A wardrobe attendant, at a lower day rate, will be hired to do any necessary clothes-pressing or repairing.

The script clerk, or script supervisor, is budgeted for the full two hours of overtime. She will be needed until the end of the shooting day to time the cleaning demonstrations and make sure that they are done in the proper amount of time.

Lines 18 through 26 of the bid form don't apply to the Cleen-Up job, but as previously mentioned, Mike does pencil in a production assistant for two pre-production days and the day of the shoot. Lines 28, 29, and 30 don't apply to this shoot, either, so Mike totals up page 1 and goes on to page 2.

The first section on page 2 is *Pre-Production & Wrap/Materials & Expenses*. For the Cleen-Up job Mike doesn't have to estimate anything for auto rentals, air fares, per diems, or still-camera rental and film. He does, however, have to include some money for messengers to carry material between the production company and the agency and between the production company and the stage. In addition, he puts in costs for trucking, to cover delivery of the set pieces; and taxis, to cover travel between the production company, the agency, and the stage.

PRE-PRODUCTION & WRAP/MATERIALS & EXPENSES	Estimated	Actual	
31. Auto Rentals (Cars @ $ x days)			
32. Air Fares: No. of people ( ) x Amount per fare ( )			
33. Per Diems: No. of people ( ) x Amount per day ( )			
34. Still Camera Rental & Film			
35. Messengers	*100*		
36. Trucking	*100*		
37. Deliveries & Taxis	*50*		
38. Home Economist Supplies			
39. Telephone & Cable	*150*		
40. Art Work			
41. Casting (*3* Days @ $*75 +)200*	*575*		
42. Casting Facilities / Equipment	*2.00*		
SUB TOTAL C	*1175*		

Then he puts in a figure to cover rental and use of phones on the stage.

The production company isn't responsible for any artwork in this job, but they have been asked to pay for a casting director and casting facilities, so these figures are added.

The next two sections of the bid form (see p. 62) deal with set construction: one covering the crew; the other, materials. Mike can't fill these out until he has called Lee, his set designer:

"Lee, what we're looking for is a country kitchen—three walls. There should be a hall on one side, where the first scene will be shot. The hall can be as simple as one 'wild' wall. [A wild wall is one that isn't permanently attached to the set and that can be moved to different locations in the set.] We also need a bathroom tile wall. Make it light in color so we can shoot a cleaning demonstration on it."

Lee makes a rough estimate of what it will cost to build the kind of set Mike has described. He has to take into consideration the size of the crew he will need to build the set and tear it down, and how much money will be required for materials. Then he calls Mike back with the breakdown and Mike records the figures on the form.

SET CONSTRUCTION (CREW FOR BUILD, STRIKE)	# MAN DAYS	Estimated	Actual	
43. Set Designer Name: *220*	4	1400		
44. Carpenters	3	415		
45. Grips	3	395		
46. Outside Props	2	270		
47. Inside Props	3	395		
48. Scenics	2	275		
49. Electricians	1	135		
50. Teamsters				
51. Men for Strike (*2* grips, *2* props, *2* elect., *1* misc.) *1 135 405*		855		
52. *+2 125 375*				
53. *PA 75*				
54.				
	SUB TOTAL D	4140		

man days ....

SET CONSTRUCTION MATERIALS	Estimated	Actual	
55. Props and Set Dressings	1700		
56. Lumber	950		
57. Paint / Wallpaper	300		
58. Hardware			
59. Special Effects			
60. Special Outside Construction			
61. Trucking	500		
62. Messengers / Deliveries	100		
63.			
SUB TOTAL E	3550		

The last section on page 2 of the bid form is *Studio Rental & Expenses—Stage*. Mike figures he will have to rent a studio for a total of four days: two to build the set; one to shoot the commercial; and one after the shoot to tear the set down. He also estimates power charges, miscellaneous studio charges, and meals. Now page 2 is complete.

STUDIO RENTAL & EXPENSES - STAGE:	Estimated	Actual	
64. Rental for Build / Strike (*2½* days @ $ *350*)	1050		
65. Rental for Pre-Lite Days (days @ $)			
66. Rental for Shoot Days (*1* days @ $ *500*)			
67. Rental for Shoot O. T. (Hrs.)	500		
68. Rental for Build / Strike Days O.T. (Hrs.)	200		
69. Total Power Charge & Bulbs			
70. Misc. Studio Charges & Service			
71. Meals (Lunches & Dinner for Crew and Talent)	400		
72.			
73.			
74.			
75.			
SUB TOTAL F	2150		

On page 3, the first section, *Location Expenses*, doesn't apply to the Cleen-Up job, since the commercial won't be shot on location in someone's home, but in a set at a studio.

LOCATION EXPENSES		Estimated	Actual	
76. Location Fees				
77. Guards				
78. Car Rentals				
79. Bus Rentals				
80. Camper / Dressing Room Vehicles				
81. Parking, Tolls, & Gas				
82. Trucking				
83. Other Vehicles A /				
84. Other Vehicles B /				
85. Special Crew Equipt. / Clothing				
86. Air Freight / Customs / Excess Baggage				
87. Air Fares: No. of people ( ) x cost per fare ( )				
88. Per Diems: Total No. man days ( ) x amt. per day ( )				
89. Breakfast: No. of man days ( ) x amt. per person ( )				
90. Lunch: No. of man days ( ) x amt. per person ( )				
91. Dinner: No. of man days ( ) x amt. per person ( )				
92. Gratuities, Tips and Misc. Outside Labor				
93. Cabs and other passenger transportation				
94. Limousines (Celebrity Service)				
95.				
96.				
97.				
98.				
99.				
SUB TOTAL G		—		

The next section of the bid form is *Equipment Rental*. Mike figures in the standard 35mm sound camera, a BNC. Then, based on his experience and his discussions with the director and cameraman, he breaks down the lighting equipment they will need.

EQUIPMENT RENTAL			
100. Camera Rental Type: *BNC*	4??		
101. Sound Rental	110		
102. Lighting Rental	350		
103. Grip / Dolly Rental	175		
104. Generator Rental			
105. Crane / Cherry Picker Rental			
106. VTR Rental			
107. Production Supplies	15?		
108.			
109.			
SUB TOTAL H	1185		

The next section is *Film Raw Stock Develop and Print*. In estimating how much film to budget, Mike tries to anticipate the creative team's needs in terms of how many times a scene might be shot. He makes allowances for the fact that there is a young child with dialogue in the commercial and that children can be unpredictable in front of the camera. In total, Mike guesses that about 2,500 feet of film will be shot, but to be on the safe side, he budgets 3,000.

FILM RAW STOCK DEVELOP AND PRINT		
110. Purchase of Raw Stock: footage amount (*3000*) x *.202* per foot	*600*	
111. Developing and Printing: footage amount (*2500*) x *.20* per foot	*500*	
112. Studio for Transfer: No. of hours ( )		
113. 16mm or 35mm Mag Stock: No. of hours (*05*		
114. Sync/Screen Dailies		
115.		
SUB TOTAL I	*1100*	

PROPS AND WARDROBE		
116. Location Props	-	
117. Costume/Wardrobe Rental & Purchase	*150*	
118. Animals & Handlers	-	
119. Wigs, Mustaches / Special Make-Up	-	
120. Color Correction		
SUB TOTAL J	*150*	

The last section on page 3 is *Props and Wardrobe.* Since the actors in the commercial will be wearing their own clothing, Mike only puts in a small amount of money to cover any items the actors might not have.

The first section on page 4 is *Director/Creative Fees.* Even though, creatively, Steve gets very actively involved in a project and meets for many hours with the agency creative/production team, he doesn't charge a fee for this pre-production time. Therefore, in this section, Mike only pencils in Steve's shooting-day rate.

DIRECTOR / CREATIVE FEES:	Estimated	Actual	
121. Prep Days			
122. Travel Days			
123. Shoot Days			
124. Post-production Days	*3000*		
125.			
SUB TOTAL K	*3000*		

The last section in the bid form that has a bearing on the Cleen-Up job is *Miscellaneous Costs.* Mike, in filling out this section, enters over $300 for petty cash to cover last-minute expenses that always crop up for another small prop, an extra roll of tape, or the like.

MISCELLANEOUS COSTS		Estimated	Actual	
126. Total Payroll & P & W Taxes	% of total of A, B, D, & K			
127. Air Shipping / Special Carriers		—		
128. Phones and Cables		*150*		
129. Misc. (Petty Cash)		*350*		
130. Misc. Trucking & Messengers		*50*		
131.				
132.				
133.				
SUB TOTAL L		*550*		

The rest of the bid form deals with areas that will be handled by the agency; so, as far as Mike is concerned, the form is finished. Now he transfers the subtotals from each section to the cost-summary page. He adds in a 35 percent markup for his overhead and profit and the grand total is his bid on the Cleen-Up commercial.

Incidentally, Mike's grand total of $28,069 doesn't represent the full amount that the commercial will cost the client. In order to arrive at the final price, inclusion must be made of the cost of editing the commercial, talent costs, and the agency's expenses and commission. The total cost to the client for the Cleen-Up commercial will be $37,500.

TELEVISION COMMERCIAL PRODUCTION

STUDIO COST SUMMARY

Production Co:		Date:	
Address:		Agency:	Agency job #
Telephone No.:	Job #	Client:	Product:
Production Contact:			
Director:		Agency prod:	Tel:
Cameraman:		Agency art dir:	Tel:
Set Designer:		Agency writer:	Tel:
Editor:		Agency Bus. Mgr:	Tel:
No. pre-prod. days	pre-light/rehearse	Commercial title:	No. Length:
No. build/strike days	Hours:	1.	
No. Studio shoot days	Hours:	2.	
No. Location days	Hours:	3.	
Location sites:		4.	
		Agency supplies:	

SUMMARY OF ESTIMATED PRODUCTION COSTS

1. Pre-production and wrap costs	Totals A and C	1790			
2. Shooting crew labor	Total B	2927			
3. Studio costs: Build / shoot / strike	Totals D, E, and F	9840			
4. Location travel and expenses	Total G				
5. Equipment costs	Total H	1185			
6. Film stock develop and print: No. feet	Total I	1100			
7. Props, wardrobe, animals	Total J	150			
8. Director/Creative fees	Total K	3000			
9. Payroll taxes, P & W and misc.	Total L	557			
10. Insurance		250			
11.	Sub-Total - Direct costs	20792			
12. Mark-up (% of direct costs)		7277			
13. Talent costs and expenses	Total M and N				
14. Editorial / Videotape	Total O and P				
15.	Grand Total	28069			
16. Weather day					
17.					
18.					

Comments:

9. *Casting*

At the same time that the bidding process begins, the agency creative/production team turns its attention to casting the parts for their commercial. What kind of people do they want? How old should they be? Do they speak lines or do they just have to look right for the part? A good cast is as important to a commercial as the script itself, but how do you find the right actors? This is where a specialist in that area comes in—the casting director.

A casting director is, in many ways, like a matchmaker. She brings together the talent for the commercial and the agency team producing it. A casting director is a walking talent-computer knowing which actors are available for any given part and keeping in constant touch with the talent agents who represent them. She sees a lot of theater—and not just on Broadway. Often she finds great new talent performing in small workshop productions way off Broadway.

A good casting director also spends a lot of time going to movies and to high school and college theatrical productions looking for new talent. Rarely can she go out to dinner without noticing someone in the restaurant who looks physically right for a part she has cast in the past or might cast in the future. In fact, a good casting director is mentally casting day and night, even when she isn't working on a specific project.

When she has time between casting jobs, a casting director makes appointments to see the hundreds of actors she doesn't know who have been writing and calling to meet her. This can be a very important period for her because during it she finds out what new talent is available. Sometimes she just interviews the actors for the purpose of getting to know them a bit, to see what they look like, and to find out what acting experience they've had. Other times she may have them read a script or even make a recording on videotape for her files.

Most advertising agencies in New York have their own casting departments, with several casting directors. Some, however, prefer to use outside casting services on a job-to-job basis. For the Cleen-Up commercial, the agency is using an outside casting director named Sally.

Sally studied speech and theater at UCLA, but never graduated; she married in her junior year and moved with her husband to New York. After raising two kids, Sally decided that she wanted to have a career, so she apprenticed herself to one of the large casting companies in Manhattan. She worked there for several years, advancing steadily from receptionist to assistant casting director to casting director. Finally, when she felt she had the necessary experience and contacts, she opened her own small casting service.

To start the casting process, JoAnne, the producer, sends Sally a copy of the storyboard. Then she calls Sally to discuss the job from the talent point of view. While they talk, Sally may fill out a casting specification sheet that will contain, when completed, all the data she requires for making her casting decisions.

First, Sally needs some general information. What company is sponsoring the commercial and what product is the commercial advertising? She has to know this because there is a union rule prohibiting an actor from taking a role in a commercial if he is already in another one for a competitive product. Sally also has to know how long the commercial will be on the air and whether the agency plans to use it only in selected areas around the country or nationally on the networks. This information indicates the amount of money an actor could earn from the commercial and the amount of time he will be obligated to the product.

Once Sally has this general information, she and JoAnne talk about the various roles in the commercial and the types of actors the agency team is looking for. The Cleen-Up commercial has three actors on camera and a voice-over announcer for the demonstration sequence in the middle and the product shot at the end. The announcer is called "voice-over" because he is not seen on film. Rather, his voice is heard speaking about the product, as beauty shots of the product or product demonstrations are being shown.

Sally: "Let's talk about the on-camera talent first."

JoAnne: "Okay. We'd like the mother to be between twenty-eight and thirty-five. We're looking for someone with a little personality and a lot of warmth."

Sally: "A Florence Henderson or Shirley Jones type?"

JoAnne: "Right. Her friend should be in the same age range."

Sally: "How about giving Mom's friend some character?"

JoAnne: "We don't want to go too far."

Sally: "I know, but if we can come up with someone with a little edge to her personality, it could make that scene come off with more energy."

JoAnne: "Try it and we'll see how it works. But also bring in some actresses who have a personality more similar to the mother."

Sally: "Okay. I see the little girl has lines to say. How old do you want her?"

JoAnne: "It would be great if you could find one who is eight but looks five or six. In any case, she has to look young. And please be sure that she isn't too precocious!"

Sally: "Fine. Now what about your voice-over announcer?"

JoAnne: "We'd like someone who comes off with warm author-
  ity."
Sally: "When do you want to start?"
JoAnne: "As soon as you can put it together."

The casting process itself involves several steps. First, the
casting director draws on her memory bank, her extensive files,
and the talent agents she feels handles the type of actors needed
for the commercial. From these sources she selects ten to
twenty qualified actors for each part, and appointments are
made for them to come to the casting studio.

At the studio, the actors are given a copy of the script to
study. Then they are asked to perform the parts in front of a
videotape camera. During this session, the casting director
directs the actors, trying to elicit from them their best readings,
and several different approaches to the copy may be explored.

This part of the process can take several days, depending on
the number of parts being cast. At the end of each day the casting tapes are sent to the agency where the creative/production
team reviews them and selects the best two or three actors for
each part. Then, once the team has hired a director, these
actors are invited to come to the agency for final casting.

At this point the casting director stands by waiting for the
production process to proceed along its natural course and for
the agency team to come to a decision about the actors. This
could take one or two weeks from the time the casting tapes are
sent to the team for their initial review.

When the final selections are made and the cast is approved
by the client, the casting director calls the actors' agents and
books them for the day the commercial will be shot.

10. *Pre-Production*

Pre-production is the period—usually from ten to fifteen working days—between client approval of the storyboard and the actual shooting of the commercial; it is the most critical period in the life of a commercial. During this time, the job is bid and awarded to a director, the production company puts the wheels of production in motion, and casting decisions are made. Also, during this time, the set is designed and built, and the wardrobe and props for the commercial are approved and purchased.

Pre-production is a time for preparation by all the people involved in the shooting of a commercial. How smoothly the job goes in production is directly related to how well the pre-production has gone.

AWARDING THE JOB

It normally takes three days for the production companies to complete their bid forms for a commercial and get them back to the agency. When all are in, they are analyzed by the producer and the agency business-affairs people. The agency checks to see which company has the most efficient way of producing the commercial, and in most cases, the job is awarded to the company with the lowest bid. Occasionally, however, a company other than the low bidder may recommend a different approach to the job which, though it may cost a little more, should result in a better commercial.

When the bids for the Cleen-Up commercial were compared, it was noted that MS Productions was $3,000 higher than the lowest bidder. In analyzing the bid, however, JoAnne found that they were planning a ten-hour shooting day, as opposed to only an eight-hour day for the low bidder. Because of the amount of time it might take to film the cleaning demonstrations, JoAnne felt more comfortable with a ten-hour day. She also felt it was worth the extra $3,000 to get the two hours of overtime, so she recommended MS Productions to the creative team.

Ritchie, the writer, and Charlie, the art director, agreed with JoAnne. They also felt better with a ten-hour day and agreed that the director, Steve, would do a good job with their commercial.

The price that the agency receives from the production company is called the "net" price. To this price, as explained previously, is added the cost of editing the commercial, talent costs and the agency expenses and commission. The resultant total—which, in the case of the Cleen-Up "Helping Hand" commercial, comes to $37,500—is called the "gross" price; this is what the client will have to pay.

The gross production price was presented to Jack, the client's brand manager. The agency explained why it was recommending MS Productions over the lowest bidder, and Jack accepted their recommendation. MS Productions, then, was awarded the job.

MEETING WITH THE DIRECTOR

As soon as a job is awarded, the producer schedules a meeting between the creative/production team and the director. It is important that the director understand fully what the agency wants to accomplish in the commercial so he can make it happen on film. Thirty seconds goes by very quickly and all the elements of production—from the sets to the lights to the direction of the actors—must fit together to support the advertising message.

When the Cleen-Up commercial was bid, JoAnne had talked with the production company in general terms about the set. Now she, Ritchie, and Charlie talk specifics with Steve. How should the action flow? What type of people live there? What mood do they want to create? All these things have a bearing on the set.

If it is important in a scene for a character to move from one part of the set to another, Steve must know this so he can communicate it to the set designer. He has to be told what kind of people live in the set and what mood the agency wants the commercial to convey, so he can help the designer create the proper environment.

The discussion about the mood of the commercial involves more than the set; it also indicates to Steve the kind of lighting to use. If the agency team wants to create a dramatic feeling, "source" lighting may be in order. This is strong lighting from one direction, such as sunlight streaming in through a window or intense light coming from a single lamp in a room, with gentle, less harsh light coming from another direction. This style of lighting creates heavy shadows on the actors and in the set. If, on the other hand, the team wants to create a warm feeling, Steve may recommend soft lighting, which would bathe the set in gentle light and eliminate a lot of shadows.

Steve and the agency team also discuss in detail the drama in the commercial. How do Ritchie and Charlie want the scenes to play? What kind of relationship should there be between the mother and her little girl? How close is the friendship between Mom and Helen?

Ritchie: "Basically, we want to create a warm feeling between the characters. The viewer should easily recognize the situation and like the characters in the commercial. We'd like Mom to come off as a confident and competent woman who isn't going to let a dirt smudge on a wall or a dirty counter-top get her down."

Steve: "What about the relationship between Mom and Helen?"

Ritchie: "Let's say they've known each other for years. They like each other and both have a good sense of humor."

Steve: "How do you see Mom delivering her opening line to the little girl?"

Ritchie: "I don't think there should be any reprimand in her voice, just confidence that the product is going to work."

Steve: "Okay. Now let's talk about the opening for a minute. On the storyboard you've drawn a close-up of the little girl's hand in frame one and indicated a camera pullback to include Mom. What would happen if we started out a little looser by framing the shot so we see more of the little girl, not just her hand? That will help establish the situation early, and give us a chance to see the little girl's expression as she delivers her line."

Charlie: "What would her action be?"

Steve: "Just what you have boarded. She'd take her hand off the wall, look at her mother, and say her line."

Charlie: "Will we be able to see the handprint on the wall?"

Steve: "Yes, I think we'll be able to see it."

Ritchie: "Steve, you realize it's important that we establish the dirt problem up front?"

Steve: "I understand. But this way we can also build in some of the warm relationship you're looking for."

JoAnne: "Is there time for the little girl to take her hand off the wall, look at the dirt on the wall, and then at her mother to deliver her line?"

Steve: "I think that would work."

Charlie: "I like that because showing the little girl's reaction to the dirt on the wall will help establish the relationship between her and her mother. And having her look at the wall first will help the viewers focus on the dirt itself. We just have to be sure that the dirt can be seen clearly."

Steve: "Right. Now what do you have in mind in terms of the set?"

Charlie: "We like your idea of a hall for the opening scene. As for the kitchen, it should be bright and cheerful-looking. It shouldn't be too upscale, but we'd like the feeling that there is room to move around. We were thinking in terms of a country-kitchen type."

This meeting is a briefing for the director. When he leaves, he will have the background necessary to move the production forward. He is now able to talk intelligently with his production manager about the specifics of the job. He can meet with his set designer and give him the necessary information for designing and building the proper set. And he will be able to have a meaningful discussion with his cameraman about the lighting for the commercial and any special camera moves that will be necessary.

HIRING THE CREW

As soon as the job is awarded to the production company, the production manager goes into action. He has only a short time to put the shoot together.

The first thing he does is hire the crew. Every good production manager has his little black book with the names and phone numbers of crew members he considers to be the best in the business. If people he has worked with before—people who he knows work well together and with the director—are available, he will hire them, for a good crew can help make the difference between a shoot that comes in on budget and one that runs into overtime and severe budget problems.

Next he contacts the cameraman and books him for the day of the shoot. He also sets up a meeting with the cameraman and the director a day or two before the shoot to discuss lighting and camera moves.

Then the production manager contacts the set designer and arranges for him to meet with the director; this meeting usually takes place as soon as the director gets back from the agency meeting. The production schedule for a commercial is always tight, therefore the set designer must begin work as soon as possible.

DESIGNING THE SET

The set designer—who, for the "Helping Hand" commercial, will be Lee—creates the environment within the commercial. He designs the rooms in which the action takes place and the colors he chooses for the walls and the materials he uses in the set are important factors in establishing the tone and mood of the advertising.

In the meeting that Mike has arranged, Steve explains to Lee the agency's concept of the commercial. Then, because it is important in designing a good set, Lee asks for specific information about where the actors are going to be in the set, what their action is, and where Steve wants to put his camera to photograph the action. A well-designed set not only makes the director's job of shooting a commercial easier, but helps the actors get more of a feeling for the parts they are playing.

Steve: "What we're looking for is a warm country kitchen."
Lee: "What about the woman who lives there?"
Steve: "The agency says she is a 'confident' and 'competent' woman."
Lee: "That means we'll have a well-organized kitchen with everything neatly in place. Do you want a window over the sink?"
Steve: "Yes, that will give me a light source for the scene. By the way, this should be a modern kitchen with built-in oven and a countertop range."

Country-kitchen set design for Cleen-Up commercial. Note wild wall used to create illusion of hallway. (*Robert L. Ramsey, set designer*)

Lee: "What color is the product? We don't want it blending into the background colors."

Steve: "The package is yellow, but it's bright and should stand out pretty well."

Lee: "Good. How about using dark wood cabinets with earth tones on the walls?"

Steve: "Okay, but we want the set warm and not too dark."

Lee: "I understand. I see you need a dinette set in the kitchen. Do you want a counter separating it from the sink?"

Steve: "No. One of the actors has to cross from the sink area directly to the table. There won't be time in the scene for her to walk around a counter."

Depending on how complicated the sets are, the set designer will have a sketch for the director within a day or two. If the director likes what he sees, he takes the sketch to the agency team for their reaction.

FINAL CASTING

Three to six days before the shoot, the director and the agency creative/production team attend final casting. This is the last audition for the commercial and from this session the director and agency team will select their cast.

In this final casting session the director works with the actors to find out what kind of range they have and how well they take direction. He and the agency people make their decision based on physical appearance and ability, and their choice is shown to the client on videotape at the pre-production meeting the next day.

For most actors any audition is nerve-racking, but final casting is the worst. Let's pretend one of those being auditioned is Judy. She enters a small studio at the agency and immediately feels as though she's being put under a microscope. She is asked to stand in front of a videotape camera with the actress who is reading the other part in the scene, and the bright lights shining directly in her face are blinding. This is it. If she does well, if she sells herself, if the agency team and the director like her—

she could be hired for the part. Even though she's a professional and has been through this countless times before, her throat always gets a little dry. She tries to stay loose, make a joke with her acting partner.

Steve comes around the lights toward her. "Hi," he says, "let me explain what we're doing here. This is a scene between Mom and her friend Helen. Helen is going to give a party and wants Mom to help. The joke is that the help Mom offers is her bottle of Cleen-Up. Now, you, Judy, will play Mom; and Chris, please play Helen. Any questions?"

"What is their relationship?" Judy asks.

"These two women have been friends for years. They have a warm, kidding type of relationship. Okay, let's try one."

Judy reads the lines with Chris. They've known each other for several years from other auditions, which makes it easier to get into the scene. During the final casting they aren't asked to move around much, but simply stand in front of the camera and read the lines.

"That's fine," says Steve. "Let's do one more, okay? This time, Judy, don't sell so hard on the Cleen-Up line. Make it more of a joke. And Chris, see if you can have a little more fun with the line where you try to get Judy to come over and help with the party."

Judy is beginning to feel more comfortable. She does the scene again. It flows better and she feels better, but was it good enough?

"Okay, that's all. Thank you, that was very good. We'll let you know."

Judy leaves the casting session with Chris. Did she get the part? She'll probably have to wait until that night to find out. In the meantime she has three more auditions to get through.

THE PRE-PRODUCTION MEETING

The pre-production meeting is the most important one between the time the commercial is approved for production and the shooting day. It takes place from two to five working days before the commercial is to be shot and brings together the brand manager from the client (in the case of Cleen-Up, this would be Jack); the account executive (Sandra), the creative team (Ritchie and Charlie), the producer (JoAnne) from the agency; the casting director (Sally); and the director (Steve) and his staff from the production company. The producer is the chairman of the meeting and all areas of production will be discussed and agreed to.

Casting is the first point on the agenda. The recommended actors are shown on videotape and if the client has no objections, they are approved. At this point the casting director leaves the meeting to call the agents and book the actors for the day of the shoot.

Then the producer talks about wardrobe—what the actors should be wearing in the commercial. Since the "Helping Hand" commercial takes place inside a home during the day, the actors will be dressed in casual but neat clothes. The little girl will wear a pair of jeans and a top, and the two women will wear well-fitting slacks and blouses. All the actors will be asked to bring their clothes from home the day before the shoot for the group's approval.

Next the producer presents the set sketches and explains them to the client. If there is no disagreement about these, the set designer leaves the meeting to go to the stage where the sets are to be built to oversee their construction.

Then the producer turns the meeting over to the writer and the art director for a discussion about the frame-by-frame objectives; that is, what the agency team would like to accomplish visually in each frame as they move from the storyboard to film.

Charlie: "In frames one and two we will establish dirt on the wall and the warm relationship between the little girl and her mom. Mom should be played with warm confidence and she doesn't show any anger toward the little girl. In frame three we will see how fast the product works by showing a close-up of the wall being cleaned. Frame four is a close-up of the product and we'll move into the label—"

Jack: "Excuse me, Charlie, but will the bottle be in Mom's hand?"

Charlie: "No. We were thinking it would work better if it was in limbo. That means shooting the product in no environment. In other words, there would be no background at all, just the product in a pool of light."

Jack: "But in frame three we see the bottle in Mom's hand, don't we? So wouldn't it be smoother to move in on that bottle instead of cutting away to limbo?"

Charlie: "What do you think, Steve?"

Steve: "Jack has a good point. If we move in on the bottle in Mom's hand, it would be smoother."

Charlie: "JoAnne?"

JoAnne: "I agree."

Charlie: "Okay, we'll move in on the bottle in Mom's hand and forget the limbo shot. Frame five will be a quadra-split. That means we will split the screen into quarters and show a cleaning demo in each one. We come out of the demos in frames six and seven and establish Mom and her friend Helen in the kitchen. We'll introduce the product at the end of frame seven, and frame eight will be a shot of the product on the table where Mom left it."

Next Steve describes to Jack how he would like to accomplish the objectives:

Steve: "Frame one of the storyboard is drawn with a close-up on the dirty wall. I think we should start looser than that to include the little girl's face."

Jack: "Will we be able to see the dirt on the wall?"

Steve: "I'll frame the shot so the dirt is clearly visible. We'll also have the girl look at the wall first, then move to Mom to deliver her line. That way, we can begin to establish the relationship early. If we start too close on the wall, you won't see the little girl until the end of her line."

Jack: "Okay."

Steve: "The middle sequence is pretty self-explanatory. The camera will get close to the dirt, but not so close that you lose a sense of where the demos are taking place."

Jack: "Where are they taking place?"

JoAnne: "I can answer that, Jack. As we discussed, the first demo with the little girl and Mom will be on a wall in the hall adjacent to the kitchen. The other four demos will take place in different areas: one will be on the stove in the kitchen; one on the kitchen floor; one on another wall—but not in the kitchen, maybe near a door; and the last one will be on bathroom tile."

Jack: "Thank you, JoAnne. . . . I'm sorry, Steve; please go on."

Steve: "I would like to shoot the scene between Mom and Helen in one continuous take."

Jack: "Will we be close enough to the women to see the bottle clearly at the end of the scene?"

Steve: "I'll design a camera move that will get us close to the table when Mom sits down."

Jack: "Sounds good."

After the discussion of frame-by-frame objectives, JoAnne goes over the production schedule. The "Helping Hand" commercial will be shot on a stage on the far West Side of Manhattan in three days. Five days after the shoot, the team should have the film edited and ready to show to Jack. If everything goes well, the commercial will be on the air ten days after Jack's final approval.

Once everything has been covered and the brand manager has no further questions, the meeting is adjourned. Now the commercial is in the hands of the agency creative/production team, and the director and his crew.

COUNTDOWN TO THE SHOOT

The set sketch for the Cleen-Up commercial has been approved, the actors have been booked, and the crew has been hired for the shoot day. Now Mike must see to it that everything and everyone shows up at the proper time and place. He calls all the crew members to give them their "call" (the time they are expected to be at the stage for the shoot day). He has a meeting with Pete, the cameraman, to go over the equipment he will need to get the proposed shots; then he makes arrangements to see that the necessary equipment is on the stage the day of the shoot. In commercial production, time is money, and getting equipment that has been forgotten can take a lot of time out of the shooting day.

Two days to go. . . .

Lee is working with the carpenters on the stage building the set. Mike is in constant touch about costs to see that the set doesn't go overbudget. He visits the stage from time to time to answer any questions that might arise and to make sure that the set is being built as Steve has interpreted it.

The Cleen-Up shoot is only two days away and the product hasn't shown up yet. JoAnne gets on the phone to Jack to ask where it is. She is assured that the product is on the way and should be at the stage by that afternoon or the next morning at the latest.

JoAnne, Ritchie, Charlie, Steve, and Mike meet to go over props. This isn't really a problem area for this shoot because all they're looking for is a nice, warm, lived-in-looking kitchen. What they need are the small touches. Pictures drawn by the kids on the refrigerator, the dog's food and water dishes on the floor in the background, the toaster/oven and coffee maker on the counter.

It's five o'clock and the product still hasn't shown up.

One day to go. . . .

Mike arranges for the camera equipment and lights to be delivered to the stage that afternoon. The set will be ready by four o'clock, and he wants to move the equipment in so they can get an early start the next morning.

JoAnne, Ritchie, Charlie, and Steve go over wardrobe with the stylist and actors. The clothes Judy has brought are fine; but Charlie doesn't like Chris's blouse, so the stylist is sent out to buy one in the style and color that Charlie wants. The little girl will wear her own jeans and a pullover.

The product still hasn't arrived. Another call is made to the client and again assurances are given that it will be there by early afternoon.

An important member of the production team joins the crew at this time, the A.D. (assistant director). He will become the head of the crew on the shoot day and will work with the director to see that things run smoothly. By union rule, the A.D. must join the team no later than one day before the shoot.

At four o'clock JoAnne, Ritchie, Charlie, and Steve meet at the stage to look at the set. The walls are up, but they aren't papered or painted yet. Steve walks the team through the set, explaining how it will look. They discuss the lighting. Everything seems fine—except the product still hasn't arrived.

Steve: "Can we send someone to buy the product at a store?"
JoAnne: "The bottles in the stores have the old label. That's why Jack was sending it."
Ritchie: "Can someone go pick it up from Jack?"
JoAnne: "I'll call and see—it sure is getting late."

Five o'clock. There's no product available at the client's office. They don't know what could have happened to the truck that was to deliver the product.

The walls are being painted and papered. They will be finished in another hour.

The camera equipment and lights are delivered from the rental company.

5:30 P.M.

The product finally arrives. There was a mix-up at the plant and the order didn't go out until late that morning.

6:00 P.M.

The men are done with the walls. The equipment has been placed on the set. The product and the props are there. Everything is ready for the shoot the next day.

11. *Shooting Day*

It is 8:30 A.M., and the sound stage, which is really nothing more than a large warehouse, is beginning to come to life. Coffee is perking and a table has been set up in one corner with juice and donuts.

The country-kitchen set has been built at one end of the stage, with the small hall attached to the left. It looks cold and flat in the glare of the overhead work lights.

In the set two gaffers, one in jeans and the other in painter's pants, are struggling to hang a large light from the scaffold in the ceiling. Ropes are attached to hooks in each side of the light and it is hauled upward. Once the light is secured, they begin working on another, smaller light that will be attached to the top of one of the walls of the set. One of the gaffers climbs a ladder and nails a bracket to the wall. His partner hands him the light and he slips it into the bracket.

The prop man, also in jeans and sneakers, begins propping the kitchen. He puts some pictures that could have been drawn by an eight-year-old on the refrigerator door. Then he unpacks a Mr. Coffee coffee maker and puts it on the counter near the double oven/stove. Pot holders are put on magnetic hooks and attached to the top oven.

The two sound men are unpacking their equipment near the right side of the set. One of them, in his fifties, is a veteran of over twenty-five years in the business. His partner is much younger and has been working sound for only two years.

"How should we mike this job?" the younger one asks.

"I think a fish pole will work best."

A slender microphone is taken out of its case and attached to the end of an expandable metal rod; this is the "fish pole" that will be held over the actors' heads by one of the sound men.

The grips are moving the dolly into position in the set. As soon as they've done so, they help the assistant cameraman mount the heavy camera on the front of the dolly. They watch small leveling bubbles on the side and back of the camera to make sure that it is mounted perpendicular to the ground. If the camera isn't "square" to the ground, the shots will all be at an angle and the scenes will come out lopsided.

Once the camera is mounted, the assistant cameraman loads the film magazines that will be used. Each magazine holds 1,000 feet of 35mm film, which is ten minutes of shooting time. During the ten-hour shooting day, only about twenty to thirty minutes of film will actually be shot. The rest of the time will be spent setting up shots, lighting, and rehearsing.

In a chair near the set, Dale, the script supervisor, a warm, friendly woman in her mid-thirties, is going over the script. She is timing each scene with her stopwatch so she will know how long each can take. It is her responsibility to see that when the commercial is edited, the scenes fit together and the total time is no more than twenty-eight and a half seconds. This allows for the one and one-half seconds needed in every piece of film for the pull-up* and fade-out.

In all, there are twenty-one professional crew people on the stage, all sufficiently skilled to back up the requests and needs of the director. Randy, the assistant director, will be running the

---

* In film, the sound is a little over a second ahead of the picture that goes with it. This means that a second of silent action is needed before dialogue can begin. This silent action is called "pull-up."

set for Steve. He will consult Steve about any problems or details that might arise unexpectedly, and see to it that the actors and crew are where they should be.

Steve, dressed in a workshirt and blue jeans, is near the coffee table talking to Pete, the cameraman for Cleen-Up. During the shooting day, Steve will work very closely with Pete, telling him where he wants each shot set up and how he sees the action flowing. The day before the shoot, Steve spent time on the set going over in his own mind how he plans to direct the commercial. He acted out the parts himself to see how much time it takes to wipe a wall or to cross from the kitchen counter to the table. Then he made a shot list, stating exactly what the camera would shoot during the day and which shots would be first. A good director doesn't walk on the set the day of the shoot and say to himself, "Let's see, what are we going to do here today?" He knows beforehand where the camera will be, the shooting sequence, what camera moves will take place, and what action he wants.

The day of the shoot the director sets the tone for the production. In a very real sense he is like the captain of a ship. He must be a strong leader and let his crew know exactly what he wants, when he wants it, and how he wants it done. A good director must also work well with the actors, making them feel comfortable and being able to interpret the scene for them so that they understand what they are supposed to do in order to deliver a warm, believable performance.

The cameraman has two responsibilities on the set. First, he supervises the lighting. Working with the gaffers, he sees to it that the lighting creates the mood wanted by the director and agency. Secondly, he operates the camera. He must make sure that he is capturing on film what the director has rehearsed.

Pete asks Steve where he wants to start shooting.

Steve: "We'll start in the hall with Mom and the little girl. It's not a very wide shot and we have to see a handprint on the wall."

Pete: "It's not going to be easy to light that wall so you can see the dirt and not wash out the actors' faces."

Steve: "Maybe we could use the wall to help bounce light on their faces."

Pete: "Good idea. Is the propman going to put the dirt on the wall?"

Steve: "No. A technical expert from the client will be coming for that. I told him to be here by nine o'clock."

Pete: "Okay. I'll begin roughing in the lighting now and fine-tune it when he gets the dirt on the wall."

JoAnne arrives wearing the uniform of the day—blue jeans and sneakers. She asks about the cast, and Steve tells her that the women, Judy and Chris, are in the dressing room, but that Suzy, the little girl, isn't due until nine.

As the agency producer, JoAnne's main responsibility on the day of the shoot is to make certain that everything planned for the shoot and agreed to by the client, is shot. During the day she will be observing every move on the set. She will be at the director's side all the time, watching the blocking of scenes, checking the timing, concerning herself with all the aspects of the shoot. Are the lines being delivered properly? Is the director getting the best performance from the actors? Is the staging working as it was planned and, if not, how should it be changed?

The producer is also a conduit of information to the director. Throughout the day JoAnne will talk with the creative team and the client to find out if they have any comments or questions about how the shoot is going. She then relays this information to the director. It is important that this single line of communication be maintained, for if all the agency and client people felt free to talk to the director at any time, he would become confused, not knowing whom to listen to; further, these interruptions could cause the production to run into serious overtime.

9:30 A.M.

By now, the rest of the agency team and the client people have arrived.

During the day Ritchie and Charlie will act as a barometer for Steve. They will indicate to him, through JoAnne, when they feel he is on the right track with the talent performances. Also, along with JoAnne, they will approve his choice of camera angles and moves.

On the other hand, Sandra, the account executive, and Jack, the brand manager, won't play active roles on the set. Their function will be merely to observe the proceedings. If they should have a question or comment, they will make it quietly to JoAnne.

There is an important member of the client team on the Cleen-Up set—the technical dirt expert. Most manufacturers, when shooting demonstrations for a commercial, want to show a real and fair demonstration of their product. If the advertising is talking about cleaning dirt off a wall, then they will create the kind of dirt the average housewife would be expected to clean off her wall—not a simple light dust dyed to look like mud. It does the manufacturer no good to fake a demonstration of his product's performance. If the product won't perform at home the way the television advertising promised it would, the consumer won't buy it again.

10:30 A.M.

Pete has finished lighting the first scene in the hall and is now sitting on the dolly behind the camera. JoAnne and the creative team are standing next to the camera, watching Steve rehearse the scene with Judy and Suzy.

Steve: "Suzy, when I say 'action,' I want you to look first at the handprint on the wall and then to Judy and say your line. Okay?"

Suzy: "Okay."

Steve: "And—action!"

Suzy [*looking first at the wall and then to Judy*]: "I'm sorry, Mommy."

Steve: "That's fine, Suzy. But now you have to make me believe you're sorry."

Suzy: "Okay. Can I try it again?"

Steve: "Sure. This time let's take it through the end of the scene."

Suzy looks at the wall, then at Judy, and delivers her line, more convincingly this time. Judy responds with her line and sprays the wall with the product.

Steve: "That's fine, we'll do it just that way. Pete, how did it look in the camera?"

Pete: "It looked fine."

Steve: "JoAnne, I want to shoot the whole first scene from this position. Then I'll cover the cleaning shot again in a close-up. Is that going to be a problem?"

JoAnne: "I don't think so. We'll just have to put more dirt on the wall after every take."

Steve: "Right. Let's get some more dirt on the wall and make pictures."

Another handprint is put on the wall while the agency group and the client take positions near the camera so they can watch the scene. The assistant director takes the clapstick and stands in front of the camera.

"Quiet, everyone; this is a take."

The stage becomes very still and all attention is focused on the area in front of the camera.

"Roll sound!"

The sound man turns on the tape recorder.

"Speed!"

Then the assistant cameraman pushes the button on the camera.

"Mark it!"

The assistant director raises the clapstick.

"Cleen-Up—Helping Hand—scene one-oh-one—take one."

Bang! The clapstick is clapped. The stage is quiet as Steve gives the actors their final direction. "Okay. Now, remember, Suzy, look at the wall, then at Judy. And—action!"

Through the camera lens Pete watches Suzy in close-up.

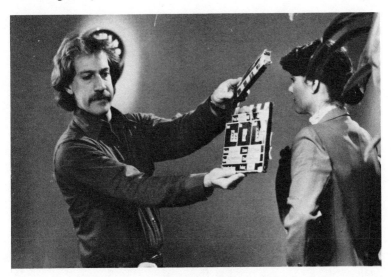

The assistant director raises the arm of the clapstick for scene 101. (*Photograph by Peter Scheer, courtesy of Schulman-Berry-Kramer Productions, Inc.*)

She looks at the wall and he begins to widen the shot. By the time Suzy looks at Judy, the shot is wide enough to show both of them in the frame. Judy says her line and cleans the wall.

Steve: "Cut!"

The camera and tape recorder are turned off.

Steve: "Suzy, that was fine, honey. But try not to smile at the beginning. Let's try it again."

Take two.

Steve: "It was almost right that time; but Judy, turn your head a little more to the light on your right so I lose the shadow on your face."

These small details can make the difference in the finished film between a shot that works and one that doesn't. Often a single five-second scene will be repeated as many as twenty times until the director feels it is perfect.

Take three.

Steve: "That was perfect, beautiful! How was it for time, Dale?"
Dale: "It ran a half second long, Steve."
Steve: "Okay. Let's do it again. Judy, I think you can pick up a half second on your line."

Take four.

Dale: "That was fine for time."
Steve: "Thanks, Dale. Judy, that was fine for time, but you looked a little awkward handling the product."

Take five.

Dale: "Steve, Suzy looked at the camera."

Take six.

Steve: "Judy, you didn't get the whole handprint off the wall. And the scene is getting a little stiff. I don't get the feeling that you love Suzy. Remember, you're not mad at her."

Take seven.

Steve: "Nice; that was very nice. Judy, I liked that warm smile you gave Suzy. What do you think, JoAnne?"
JoAnne: "Looked good to me. What do you think, Ritchie?"
Ritchie: "Steve, could we maybe get a little more surprise from Suzy when the product works so fast?"
Steve: "And maybe a little relief that she's not in trouble?"
Ritchie: "Yeah."
Steve: "Suzy, be surprised and happy that the wall got cleaned so fast."

They do several more takes before everything works right.

Steve: "I think we've got it. How was that for camera, Pete?"
Pete: "Looked good, Steve."

Steve: "Dale?"

Dale: "It came in right on time."

Steve: "All right, let's set up for the close-up of the cleaning demo."

12:30 P.M.

The shooting of the cleaning demonstration in the hall was finished by 11:30 A.M. The next scene scheduled to be shot will be the one at the end of the commercial between Mom and her friend. For the past hour Pete has been lighting the kitchen set where the scene will be filmed.

Lighting a set isn't as easy as turning on a switch. It is a real art, and careful attention must be paid to every detail. First of all, the cameraman must be aware of how the director wants to shoot the scene. Will the camera be static or will the director want to move it while the scene is being shot? What about the actors—do they have any action that will take them from one part of the set to another during the scene? Taking this all into account, the cameraman, working with his gaffers, aims the lights so that they will cover any action and create the desired mood.

For our commercial, Steve and the agency creative/production team want to convey the impression that this scene is taking place in the afternoon of a warm, sunny day. To help create this feeling, Pete aims a strong light through the window over the sink; this will be his "key," or main light. The key light is the main light source in a scene and is used to help model the actors and the area in which they are playing. Because it is very strong, the key light creates shadows and highlights and gives the set and actors a sculptured, three-dimensional look. But it must be balanced by softer "fill" light from the opposite direction to control the shadows and help create the proper effect.

Once Pete is satisfied with the lighting on the actors and their immediate area, he will light the background of the set. When he is finished, the total impression on film will be just what Steve and the agency are seeking.

Cameraman checking the light reading with a light meter. (*Photograph by Peter Scheer, courtesy of Schulman-Berry-Kramer Productions, Inc.*)

During the time that Pete is lighting the set, Steve is with the agency people and the client discussing how he plans to shoot the scene. "I'd like to start out fairly loose to include both Judy at the counter and Chris sitting at the table. As Judy crosses to the table, I'll truck the camera so that the shot tightens up and we end up on a fairly tight two-shot."

What Steve means by "truck the camera" is that he'll move the dolly during the shot.

Charlie: "Steve, can we put the table a little closer to the counter so Judy won't have so far to cross?"

Steve: "Not a bad idea, Charlie."

Pete: "Randy, please move the table a little closer to the counter."

Steve: "How much longer, Pete?"

Pete: "Give me about ten minutes."

Steve: "All right, but I want to start this scene before lunch."

6:00 P.M.

It has been a good day; no real problems. Steve was able to finish the scene in the kitchen before lunch and, during the afternoon shot the product shots and three of the remaining demonstrations. For the past hour he has been working on the last demonstration—the bathroom vanity top, which is being shot MOS, which means without sound. The announcer's voice will be added later.

The camera is turned on. Through the lens Pete focuses on the vanity top. The product is sprayed, a hand comes into frame and wipes the surface clean.

Steve: "Cut! How did that look, Pete?"

Pete: "Great."

Steve: "Okay, everyone, that's a wrap."

A "wrap" means that the shooting day is over. During the day Steve has directed forty-three takes and has shot 3,000 feet of film.

The crew will spend the next half hour or so taking down the lights and storing their equipment.

The film will be taken immediately to a lab for developing. Tomorrow the director and the agency creative/production team will screen the footage to make sure everything is satisfactory.

Then begins the job of editing thirty minutes of film into thirty seconds of advertising.

12. *The Editor*

The editor is responsible for cutting the thirty or so minutes of film that was shot into thirty seconds of advertising. But it's not just a matter of cutting and pasting pieces of film together. A good editor works closely with the agency creative/production team and helps them shape all the film that was shot into a selling commercial.

Frank, the editor for the Cleen-Up commercial, has been editing commercials for many years. He started out in 1964 as an office boy for the editorial department of one of the large "full service" production companies. He worked his way up to assistant editor and finally to editor, but in 1970, the production company shut down their editorial department because they found it was a luxury they could no longer afford. At that point, Frank and two of his colleagues formed a partnership and opened up their own independent editorial service, converting office space in midtown Manhattan into three small editing rooms.

Frank is an excellent editor: part technician and part creative. He knows how to cut and splice film together; but more than that, he knows how to use the tools at his disposal to enhance the selling of the product.

One of the most important tools an editor has are "opticals," or special visual effects. These can be as simple as dissolving from one scene to another; or they can be as complicated as shrinking a scene and moving it up in the television frame or blowing up a scene to bring it closer to the audience. Opticals can often make the difference between a commercial that sells and one that doesn't, and a capable editor knows when, and when not, to use them. If opticals aren't used properly, they can call attention to themselves and detract from the selling effectiveness of the commercial. Anyone looking at a commercial should not be aware of the special visual effects. Rather, they should underscore or heighten the selling message.

Sound is another important tool for the editor. By adding sounds or heightening those already in the commercial, the editor can help focus the selling message. For example, if beer brewed with mountain spring water is being sold, the sound of a bubbling spring might be added to the sound track. Or, to emphasize the "fresh air" quality of a room deodorizer, the murmur of a gentle breeze might be mixed in the sound.

THE DAILIES

The first step in editing a commercial is working with the "dailies."

After the shoot is over, the assistant cameraman sends the film to the lab. Here the film is developed in much the same way as are snapshots, except that the pictures from the negative are printed on another piece of 35mm film instead of on paper. These are the dailies.

At the same time that the film is being developed, the sound track is being transferred from ¼-inch audiotape to 35mm magnetic track (a clear piece of 35mm film in which there are magnetic strips). After the film is developed and the sound track transferred, the dailies, the 35mm sound track, and the original camera negative are sent to the editor.

As Frank works on the dailies from the Cleen-Up shoot, he sits at an editing machine called a "flatbed editor," which allows

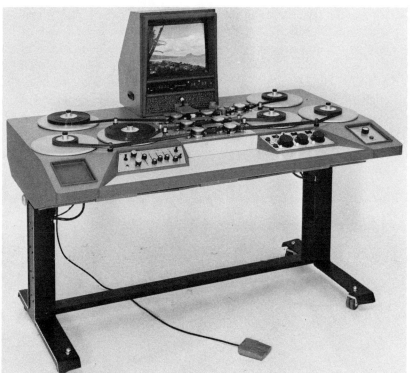

Flatbed editing machine. (*Courtesy of Magnasync/Moviola Corporation*)

him to view the film and run the sound track at the same time. A flatbed editor looks like a table with a screen attached to the back. At opposite ends of the table are three sets of plates with spindles for the reels of film and sound track. Between two sets of plates are sound heads, much like the playback head on a tape recorder; this is where the sound track goes. Between the set of plates closest to the screen is a picture head that projects the film onto the screen at the back. On a flatbed editing machine Frank can run the sound track and picture separately or he can lock them together with a sync (synchronizing) motor.

Frank is "syncing up" the dailies—lining up the pictures so that they are in perfect synchronization with the sound that goes with them. He finds the place at the beginning of each scene where the clapstick has closed and marks that precise frame of film with a grease pencil. Then he listens carefully to the sound track and marks the exact spot where the sound of the clapstick is heard. Next he lines up the two marks on his flatbed editor, engages the sync motor, turns on the machine, and the scene plays on his screen with the pictures and dialogue in perfect synchronization.

Frank has worked for an hour getting the dailies ready to be screened. When he is done, he takes them to a large screening room on Fifth Avenue for viewing by the agency team and the director.

The group screens the dailies for two reasons: first, to make sure there is nothing wrong with the film—that is, to see that there is an image on the film and that the image is in focus and not scratched; second, to enable the agency creative/production team to select what they feel are the best "takes" of each scene. (Every time a scene is shot it is called a "take.") The agency team looks at all 3,000 feet of film, sometimes as many as twenty takes per scene.

During the screening, Frank makes notes on the takes that the agency likes. When he gets back to his office, he pulls the selected takes out of the dailies and makes a special, or "select," reel. Now he is ready to begin editing the film into a commercial.

EDITING THE COMMERCIAL

Frank's editing room isn't large, but it is comfortable. At one end is a couch and a couple of director's chairs for his clients. At the other end is his flatbed editing machine, where he and JoAnne are working on the film. Next to the editing machine is a "trim barrel," which looks very much like a large garbage can lined with a cloth bag. Attached to its top is a metal frame with thin wire pegs. Once Frank begins editing, he will use the trim barrel to hold the pieces of film and sound track that he trims from a scene.

Frank has cut together two reels of the selected takes. One has all the dialogue scenes; the other, all the product shots and cleaning demonstrations that were shot without sound. He threads up the dialogue reel and sound track, and he and JoAnne screen the takes of the first scene. This scene was shot twenty times, but only five takes—7, 8, 12, 15, and 20—were considered acceptable by Steve and the agency team. What Frank and JoAnne are looking for is a take that not only conveys the most warmth between the mother and the little girl, but also shows the dirt on the wall and the product.

The machine is turned on and the five takes run through.

JoAnne: "I like take fifteen. What do you think?"

Frank: "The relationship is very warm, but did you notice that Mom is holding the product too far away and that it never really gets into frame?"

JoAnne: "Let's look at the scene again."

They run the scene from the top.

JoAnne: "You're right. The product doesn't really get established. What other take do we have that would work better?"

Frank: "How about twenty? There's warmth and you can see the product."

JoAnne: "But the end of the scene is so stagy, so flat. The mother looks as if she is an announcer selling the product instead of a mother who has the solution to a problem."

Frank: "I see what you mean. Well, there's something wrong with every take, but fifteen has the best readings by the actors and the warmest relationship."

JoAnne: "Right. So how will we solve the product-registration problem?"

Frank: "We can cut to the cleaning demonstration a little early. Steve covered the beginning of the first cleaning demo a little looser than the rest, so we get a good look at the product in Mom's hand before the wall is sprayed. After the

spray, he zoomed in a little on the wall for the wipe. We
can cut to that shot and establish the product in close-up
over Mom's line, 'I've got a helping hand.' "
JoAnne: "Let's try it."

Frank pulls take 15 out of the select reel and puts it on an
empty reel. He does the same with the sound track for the take.
Next he splices the silent footage of the demo to the end of the
take. Now he has take 15 and the demo on the same reel. This
is called his "work-print reel," because it is on this reel that he
will build the commercial. When he is through editing, the
work print will be an unpolished version (called a "rough cut")
of the commercial, with grease-pencil marks on the film to indicate where the opticals should go.

Frank puts the select reel aside and threads up his work-print
reel. He runs the scene from the beginning until he finds the
place where he wants to cut to the close-up of the product in
the demo. Then he stops the machine and marks the wanted
frame and the sound track. This is called the "cut-out point,"
because that is where he will cut out of the scene.

Frank now disengages the sync motor and, leaving the track
stationary, runs the picture through to the demo footage. He
finds the frame he wants to cut to and marks it as his "cut-in
point" (the point where he will pick up that scene). The sync
motor is engaged and Frank runs the demo footage with the
sound track from take 15. Mom says, "I've got a helping hand,"
and the picture shows a close-up of the product in her hand
next to the dirt on the wall.

The shot seems to work, so Frank rolls the demo back to his
cut-in point and actually cuts the film. Next he disengages the
sync motor again, which leaves the sound track where it is, and
rolls the film back to his cut-out point in the scene. He cuts
again, taking the unwanted footage out of the scene. This
footage, called a "trim," goes into the trim barrel. Then he
carefully splices the demo footage into the scene, using special
clear editing tape.

"Okay, JoAnne, let's see if it works."

The scene is run from the beginning, with the sound. The picture shows a close-up of the little girl and the dirt on the wall, then a pullback to show Mom. Mom starts to bring the product up into frame, and on her line about the helping hand there is a close-up of the product.

JoAnne: "That seems to work. I like the relationship between the mother and the little girl, and the close-up of the product comes in at just the right time."

Frank: "Don't you think we should stay on the demo for the little girl's line, 'Wow! That's clean!' "

JoAnne: "I don't know. I'll miss the girl's face on her line."

Frank: "But you'll get a better look at the demo itself."

JoAnne: "What would happen if we hold on the close-up for the first part of her line, then cut back to the wider shot?"

Frank: "That could work. Let's do it."

Frank edits the end of the first scene and plays it for JoAnne. The picture shows the cleaning demo while the voice of the little girl is heard saying, "Wow!" Then her face is shown as she says, "That's clean!"

Frank and JoAnne next begin working on the cleaning demonstrations in the middle of the commercial. On the announcer's line, "That's Cleen-Up . . . ," they cut from the little girl to a shot of the product. At the point where they want the demos to go, Frank makes a mark with his grease pencil to indicate that there will be a dissolve to the quadra-split screen, with a different cleaning demonstration in each of the four areas. Since a quadra-split screen is a special optical, it isn't added at this rough-cut stage. Instead, Frank cuts in only one of the demos as an example; the other three will be added at the end of the rough cut so that everybody at the agency and the client can see what they look like. Also, the dialogue for the entire middle sequence will be added later by an announcer, so to cover this sequence, Frank cuts blank film, called "leader," into the sound track.

Now work begins on the last scene—that between Mom and Helen. Frank follows the same procedure he did with the first scene—removing the work-print reel and putting up the reel of selected takes so that he and JoAnne can screen the takes for the one they feel works best.

Steve covered this scene in a master shot, which has all the action from beginning to end in one continuous take. He also covered the end of the scene in a tight two-shot, which focuses on Mom for her line, "I've got just the thing."

Frank and JoAnne agree that the master shot should be used. They find a good take and Frank cuts it into the work print. In the take, Helen is sitting at the table and Mom is by the sink, just finishing using the product. The focus of the scene is on Helen, but as Mom comes to the table with the product and sits down, the camera moves to focus on both women equally.

The commerical is now cut into rough shape, ready to be screened by Ritchie and Charlie. They sit in front of the editing machine and look at the rough cut from start to finish. Ritchie has no objections to any part of it, but Charlie has reservations about the last scene, the one between Mom and Helen. He doesn't feel the mother has the sparkle they were looking for.

Frank puts up the select reel and they look at the other master takes of the scene. Then they look at the takes of the two-shot at the end.

Charlie: "The master take we're using is the best one, but the scene just doesn't work for me this way. Let's see what happens when we cut to the two-shot."

Frank cuts the two-shot into the proper place. The beginning of the scene is the same, with Helen at the table and Mom by the sink. Mom walks to the table and, as she starts to sit, there is a cut to the tight two-shot featuring Mom for her line.

Charlie: "Much better. Now we're focused on Mom and the scene has some punch at the end."

Ritchie: "How are we on time, Frank?"

Frank: "Not bad. At this point we're about a foot long, but I can
trim some from the first scene and some at the end as we cut
to the product shot."

When Frank is done trimming the commercial to time, it
will be exactly 45-feet long (720 frames). The rough cut, with
no opticals, is now finished. The next step is to show it to the
various groups at the agency, then to the client.

13. *Screening the Rough Cut*

When the creative/production team is satisfied with the editing done on the rough cut, they take it to the agency to screen for their creative management (the copy supervisor and/or the creative director) and the account group.

Advertising is creativity by committee—the writer and art director developing the concept and writing the storyboard of the commercial; their creative management and account group making subtle changes; the client brand manager suggesting ideas on how the advertising should flow. Then there is legal input from client and agency counsel, and the invaluable perspective added by the agency producer. This is the process that the advertising goes through at the storyboard stage; it goes through almost the same process as a rough cut of the commercial.

THE AGENCY SCREENING

This screening of the rough cut is a crucial one for the creative/production team. It is at this session that they and their colleagues will discuss the type of announcer they will use, the special sound effects they plan, and exactly how and where the opticals will go. Until these agency people are in agreement, the creative/production team can't take the rough cut to the client.

The first screening is for the creative management, which is concerned, on one hand, with the look and feel of the commercial; and on the other, with the way the client's message is coming across. Creative management's primary interest is in seeing that the message is delivered in as involving and engaging a way as possible. This is not to say that the look of the film or the action in the film should take away from the message, but rather that the film should communicate its message in a creative way, and not in a pedestrian, predictable fashion.

When creative management approves the way the commercial is edited, the rough cut is screened for the account group. Their main concern is to see that the film is a fair translation of the storyboard they sold the client. They also want to assure themselves that the commercial clearly communicates the benefits of the product.

It sometimes happens that either the creative management or the account group have suggestions or questions that necessitate some more work on the rough cut. They could feel, for instance, that a reading by one of the actors was too harsh or too rushed. They may not agree with the way a scene is cut or want to see what a close-up would look like in a scene where there isn't one cut in.

If this happens, the creative/production team takes the rough cut back to the editor. They look at different takes and try to accommodate the suggested changes. Then it's back to the agency again, this time hopefully to get agreement to screen the rough cut for the client.

THE CLIENT SCREENING

Jack, the brand manager, has been waiting for this day with some anticipation. It has been four weeks since the agency got approval to produce the "Helping Hand" commercial and two weeks since the commercial was actually shot. All the reports from the agency have been good, and now he will see for himself whether or not the commercial works.

For the creative team there is a feeling of déja vu about the meeting. They are in the same conference room where they presented the original storyboard. The same feeling of nervous excitement is in the air; in fact, everything is the same as before except that instead of storyboards of the concept, they have brought a ¾-inch videocassette of the rough cut.

Just as in the copy meeting, Sandra, the account executive, makes a few opening remarks and reminds everyone why they are there. Then she turns the meeting over to Ritchie and Charlie.

"Jack," says Ritchie, "we'd like to remind you that this is a rough cut. That means that there are no opticals and we haven't recorded the announcer or mixed the sound track. In the middle of the commercial, where the special split-screen effect will go, we have put only one of the cleaning demonstrations to show you how the commercial will flow. The rest of the demos have been spliced together at the end of the commercial so you can see what they look like. Since we haven't recorded the announcer yet, JoAnne has made a scratch track, using her voice where the announcer's will be heard."

(A scratch track is a rough, temporary recording of the voice-over announcer's dialogue used to help edit film that was shot silent. It is usually made by the producer at the editor's office and is replaced by a professional announcer at the time of the sound mix.)

The button is pushed on the videocassette machine and the commercial runs from the beginning.

For a brand manager, analyzing a commercial on film is very different from analyzing a storyboard. With a storyboard he can dissect the concept, go over all the principles of copy analysis, and study the storyboard a frame at a time. A storyboard is, after all, only a flat piece of paper with pictures and words on it. Film is a very different animal and is difficult to analyze a piece at a time.

The first thing a good brand manager does is to look at the commercial once from beginning to end. He lets it wash over him and tries to take in the message as a whole, as a consumer would when seeing it for the first time. Seventy-five percent of the brand manager's overall response to the commercial should come from this first viewing. He should experience a gut reaction to whether he likes it or not, whether the selling message is coming through, and whether it's easy to understand.

After this initial look at the commercial as a whole, the brand manager will ask for a second screening. This time he will look for some specifics. Is the key visual—the visualization of the selling message—as impactful as it can be? Is the commercial paced well or is it going too fast [advertising shouldn't whiz by the viewer]? Is the acting credible—neither underplayed nor overplayed—and does it feed to the credibility of the product story? All these objectives have been discussed in the copy and pre-production meetings. Now the brand manager can see if the objectives were met.

Jack: "I like it. I think, overall, you've done a pretty good job of telling the Cleen-Up story in thirty seconds. But I'm a little bothered by the cleaning demonstrations; they go by so fast. I wonder if the viewer will get a good look at what we do?"

Sandra: "You know we're planning to put four demonstrations in a quadra-split screen. That should certainly get the message across."

Jack: "Maybe. But even the first demo with Mom and the little girl goes by pretty fast. Is there any way to make those scenes a little longer?"

Ritchie: "We can look, but I honestly don't know if that will help you, because it just doesn't take very long to clean a handprint off a wall or fingerprints from around a doorknob."

Charlie: "I have an idea—we could bump up the sound of the spray as it comes out of the bottle before each demo. What I mean is that, in the mix, we could make the sound of the spray coming out of the bottle louder than normal. That will help focus on the product just before the demo and could add some life to the spray hitting the wall or door or whatever."

Jack: "What about the shots in the split-screen? We won't even see a bottle in those shots."

Charlie: "Right. But if we establish the sound effect in the first cleaning sequence with Mom, then we can use it even without the bottle in the shot and the viewer will know what the sound is."

Jack: "Will that work?"

Charlie: "I think so. We can also look for different shots of the cleaning demonstrations. Maybe we can find shots where you see the spray hitting the surface a little better. That will make the sound more effective because you will be able to see the spray you are hearing."

Jack: "Sounds good, Charlie. Let's do it. [*He turns to Sandra.*] What are our next steps?"

Sandra: "As soon as we get your agreement, and your management's, we'll record the announcer for the demonstrations and the end tag. Then we'll mix the sound track and go to opticals."

14. Finishing the Commercial

Now we enter the last stage of the birth of a commercial: finishing it, preparing it, so it can get on the air. Once the client approves the rough cut, the agency creative/production team returns it to the editor to begin the process that will result in a finished piece of advertising. To do this the editor must polish the two separate pieces of the rough cut—the sound and the picture.

PREPARING THE SOUND TRACKS

Sound is extremely important to the finished commercial. It must not detract from the advertising, but should work with the pictures to help the consumer understand the selling message.

The editor begins by building the different pieces of the sound track. At the rough-cut stage, the only sound is the dialogue that was recorded when the commercial was shot. Now other sound tracks must be recorded for any special effects and the voice-over announcer. In all, there could be as many as fifteen different tracks for one commercial. The editor lists these tracks on a cue sheet and marks the places where each should come in and go out in order to fit with the pictures. He also indicates whether they should come in fast or slow, and whether

111

the tracks should fade from one to another (this transition is called a "segue").

The Cleen-Up commercial will have only three tracks to mix together: the dialogue track, the special-effects track for the sound of the spray, and a voice-over announcer track. Since the announcer will be recorded just prior to the sound mix, Frank, the editor, marks on his cue sheet exactly where the announcer track should go. Then he makes an effects track of the spray and notes on the sheet where it should be brought into the commercial. Now he is ready to record the announcer and mix the sound track for the commercial.

RECORDING THE ANNOUNCER

The sound studio is dimly lit. Inside voices are muffled by the soundproofing in the room. The studio is quiet and peaceful.

The front wall of the studio is really a large movie screen with a digital frame counter underneath. At the back of the room the sound mixer, Tom, is at the sound console, with its dozens of knobs, buttons, and levers. It's from here that Tom will control the sound tracks and blend them together. Frank, cue sheet in hand, sits beside him.

In front of the console are comfortable chairs, where JoAnne, Ritchie, and Charlie are sitting, watching the screen. Behind them, in a corner, is a soundproof booth where Adam, the announcer, is waiting.

JoAnne: "Adam, you have eight seconds for the middle sequence. Now don't rush. We want it nice and warm."
Adam: "Right."

Tom pushes a button that starts an unseen tape recorder. Then he points at Adam in the booth.

Tom: "Cleen-Up—take one."
Adam [*pausing to get a breath*]: "That's Cleen-Up! It's like hav-

ing a helping hand with those little cleaning chores around the house. Cleen-Up cuts through tough dirt fast and leaves surfaces shining."

JoAnne: "That was right on time, Adam, but it sounded a little flat."

They do another take and this time it is just what the agency team wants. They then record the end sequence:

Adam: "Cleen-Up! It's like having a helping hand to help clean up around the house."

JoAnne: "That's fine, Adam. Thank you."

Now they are ready for the mix.

THE MIX

In the mix all the tracks are blended together to make a new, finished sound track for the commercial. In a way it is like painting a picture in sound. Dialogue can be made louder or softer, music can be blended in under dialogue, and sound effects can be placed at the right spot to underscore the picture.

In the mix the final sound track is also equalized—balanced so that the sound level doesn't vary from scene to scene. It is possible that at the shoot the sound might have been recorded at different levels for different scenes; or, within a scene, one actor might have sounded louder than another. These sounds must be balanced to avoid having them distract from the commercial. Also, if there is some outside noise on the sound track, such as the hum of an air conditioner, it will be filtered out to make the final track as clear as possible.

During the mix, Frank fills much the same role as Steve did as the director of the shoot. Frank is responsible for supervising the sound mixer and telling him when and how the various sound tracks should be brought in. In effect, the editor directs the mix.

The sound tracks that Frank brought with him are in a separate room on large machines called "dubbers." These dubbers can be controlled from the sound console, as can the projector that will show the film. Tom makes sure that the right take of the announcer track is cued up on the dubber. Then he pushes the button to start the tape that will record the final sound track for the Cleen-Up commercial.

"Cleen-Up, 'Helping Hand,' thirty-second-mix track."

The projector is turned on in sync with the dialogue track. Just as Mom is getting ready to spray the wall, Tom starts the track of the sound effect. Before Mom pushes the button, there is a loud sound of the spray.

Frank thinks the spray sound came in too soon. Tom says he'll delay it a couple of frames. The film and sound track are run backward to the beginning. Tom pushes a button that moves the effects track back two frames, and starts the film again. The scene plays on the screen at the front of the room. This time, with the sound of the spray coming in two frames later, it appears to be in perfect sync with Mom's action.

Ritchie: "Frank, the spray is coming in at the right time, but it sounds harsh—almost like the end of a sneeze or something."

Frank: "We could take the volume down."

Ritchie: "I don't know if that will do it."

Frank: "How about filtering the sound, Tom?"

Tom: "I don't think that will help. Maybe we should try taking some of the treble off. It will make the spray sound just a little flatter, not so shrill."

Tom adjusts a knob on the console, runs the scene back to the beginning and lets it play again. This time the spray sound is gentler.

Ritchie: "That's good, Tom. That's the way it should sound for all the sprays."

An hour later they are finished; the sound is exactly as it will be heard in the final commercial, balanced from scene to scene. The announcer's voice has been mixed into the commercial at just the right places and every time the product is sprayed, the sound effect is just right. This sound track is called the "mixed mag" track, because it exists only on magnetic tape. In order to prepare the sound to join the picture on one piece of film, it must be transferred to an "optical" sound track. An optical sound track is nothing more than a picture of the sound. Sound oscillates, vibrates, and these impulses are imprinted on special film. It is like taking pictures of the sound waves of the mag track. This, then, becomes the optical sound track which is now ready to join the pictures to make the Cleen-Up commercial complete.

PREPARING THE PICTURES

The picture part of the commercial goes through several steps before it can be married to the sound track. First, however, the original negative must be "conformed" to the rough cut.

The rough cut has very small figures called "key numbers" printed on the side of the film. These run chronologically and correspond to numbers on the original negative, which has been sitting in cans, untouched, during the preparation of the rough cut.

Once the client approves the rough cut, the editor makes a list of the key numbers. Then he locates the corresponding numbers on the negative and cuts them together. Now he has created with the negative the same sequence of pictures as that in the approved rough cut.

Once the editor has conformed the original negative, he is ready to begin the optical process. He takes the film to an optical company, where he first checks to ensure that the color of the final film will be perfect; then he creates the special optical effects that will be incorporated into the commercial.

Color film analyzer. (*Courtesy of the Hazeltine Corporation*)

THE COLOR ANALYZER

The color in a commercial is checked and maintained by means of a machine called a "color analyzer," a special piece of equipment that helps balance the picture in terms of color quality and density (i.e., lightness or darkness). This is important because the color should remain the same as the commercial moves from one scene to another. For example, if an actress is wearing a blue print blouse, its color should look the same in every scene—not dark blue in one, and robin's egg blue in the

Optical printer. (*Courtesy of Oxberry*)

next. The color analyzer performs for the film roughly the same function that the equalizing of the sound track does for the mix.

The machine itself is a small table with a television screen built into the back. Set into the table are several dials that control color and density. A frame of the original negative is slipped into the machine, a picture is projected on the television screen, and the dials are manipulated to obtain the color wanted in the scene. Readings are then taken to find out how much correction is required to keep that same color quality in the rest of the scenes.

Once the color quality has been made consistent throughout the commercial, it's time to create the opticals.

THE OPTICAL PRINTER

Opticals are created on an "optical printer," a large, strange-looking machine with reels, buttons, and wires attached from seemingly every direction; it looks like one of the contraptions Dr. Frankenstein might have used to create his monster, or a piece of modern sculpture designed by Picasso. Actually, the optical printer is designed to photograph the negative of the commercial, either all at once or a frame at a time. It has two main pieces of equipment built into it: a projector and a camera.

To use the optical printer, the original negative is threaded onto the special projector. On the other end of the optical printer, facing the projector, is the special camera that can move in any direction—forward, backward, up, down, and on the diagonals. It is with this camera that all special effects for film are created.

To achieve the quadra-split-screen effect for the Cleen-Up commercial, the opening scenes are run through the optical printer and photographed as they were cut. At the place where the effect should be inserted, the camera and projector are turned off. The first frame of the first cleaning demonstration is then projected to the camera, somewhat as though it were a still photograph. By looking through a special eyepiece, Frank and the optical company personnel can see the picture and, by controlling the position of the camera in relation to the projector, place it exactly where it should go.

The first cleaning demonstration has been slated to appear in the upper-left quadrant of the television screen. When the picture has been correctly positioned, the projector and camera are turned on again and the film of the demonstration runs through. It shows the first cleaning demonstration photographed where it should be—in the upper-left corner of the film, as shown on the following page.

The camera is now backed up to the beginning of the sequence and the second cleaning demonstration is positioned in the upper-right corner. The camera and projector are turned on again and this demonstration is photographed to join the first. Now the film looks like this:

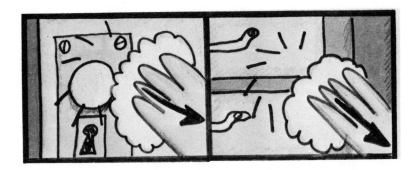

This process is repeated two more times until the quadra-split-screen effect is achieved, looking like this:

The optical printer is also used to create less-complicated effects, such as putting titles (supers) into the commercial and creating fades and dissolves. (A fade is an effect in which the picture goes from full brightness to a blackout, or vice versa; a dissolve, as explained earlier, is an overlapping of the fade-out of one scene with the fade-in of the scene following it. Thus, one scene literally dissolves into the other.)

The end result of work on the optical printer is an "optical negative." This is a negative that has all the effects, all the dissolves, all the fades and titles. The complete picture of the product's story is now on one piece of film and is ready to be joined to the sound track.

To complete the commercial, the sound (optical track) and picture (optical negative) are married on one piece of film called a "composite print." This marks the first time the entire commercial is together. If the color looks right, if the opticals appear at the right time and look the way they should, and if the sound plays in perfect sync with the pictures, the commercial is ready for the air. Copies, called "release prints," are made and distributed to stations all across the country and within weeks the "Helping Hand" commercial can be seen in living rooms from Seattle to Baltimore.

VIDEOTAPE FINISHING

Currently, most commercials are finished on film, in the way described in the foregoing pages. However, videotape cannot be ignored as another possible method of completion.

While it is true that most creative teams prefer the softer look of film for *shooting* their commercials, videotape has become an acceptable medium for *finishing* commercials. A creative team can shoot the commercial on film, edit on film, and then transfer the rough cut and mixed-mag track to tape for opticals. In fact, because of significant technological advancements in the videotape industry, it is now possible to create on tape most of the opticals that can be made on film.

Videotape-finishing has two advantages over film: (1) there is instantaneous feedback of what is being created; in other words, it's not necessary to wait for any film to be developed to see if everything is right; and (2) a commercial finished with tape can get on the air much faster. Once the opticals have been created, a tape-finished product can go on the air immediately; one that has been finished on film could take as much as two weeks longer.

If tape-finishing is faster than conventional film-finishing, and if it is true that the same use of opticals is possible, why isn't tape-finishing the predominant method for completing commercials? The answer is economics. Finishing on tape does cost more than finishing on film, but the dollar difference isn't all that significant. However, commercials finished on tape have to be distributed on tape, and tape dubs are much bulkier than those of film prints; therefore they cost considerably more to ship to television stations. On the other hand, if the costs of tape-finishing and distribution should come down, making it faster and easier than the lengthy film process to get a commercial on the air, then more and more commercials will be finished on tape.

FINALE

Four months after the copy assignment was made, the "Helping Hand" commercial was on the air across the country. In all, over thirty people had worked to bring "Helping Hand" from a concept to a finished piece of advertising. It had taken close to five hundred working hours and nearly a half mile of film, but in the end they had what they wanted—an effective thirty-second television commercial ready to help boost the sales of Cleen-Up.

15. Hidden-Camera Testimonials —the Exception to the Rule

The story of the Cleen-Up "Helping Hand" commercial is typical of the way most commercials are conceived, written, and produced. As a general rule, they all start with a creative concept which is turned into a storyboard. Next, as we have seen, the storyboard is first used as a tool to sell the client on the advertising concept and then as a guide for the production, with the pictures indicating the visual flow that the creative team has in mind, and the copy, or script, becoming the dialogue. This sequence is followed for all types of commercials—slice-of-life, animated, tabletop, or whatever—with one notable exception: hidden-camera testimonials; these follow a very different path from concept to finished advertising.

There are two major differences between hidden-camera testimonials and other forms of television advertising. For one thing, since commercials of this kind depend on the "testimony" of actual consumers, the creative team can't write dialogue or create an accurate storyboard until after the testimony is given; that is, until after the commercial is shot. Second, all other executional forms depend on professional performers speaking the dialogue written by the creative team. Testimonial advertising depends on nonprofessional "real" people expressing their own opinions about a product. This is the real strength of testimonial advertising.

Legally, hidden-camera testimonials are bound by exactly the same regulations as all other commercials in regard to claims and demonstrations. Everything a "real" person says in a commercial about a product must be true, and all demonstrations must actually work the way they appear to; if they don't, that fact must be disclosed to the person being interviewed and to the viewer.

In addition, hidden-camera commercials must adhere to one other legal requirement: *The person being interviewed must not know that his testimony could be used in advertising until after he has given it of his own free will.* The legal view is that if a consumer is told beforehand that a commercial is being made, the odds are that his testimony will be prejudiced in favor of the product in question.

It also makes sense, from a creative point of view, not to inform the people being interviewed about the possibility of their being in a television commercial. If they are used, they should come across in as natural a way as possible, and this is not likely to happen if they know they are being filmed. Instead, they will probably appear nervous, their remarks will seem forced, and they will be totally unbelievable.

To illustrate how a hidden-camera commercial is developed and produced, let's assume that Cleen-Up has just developed a new, improved product. The new product has better grease-cutters than the original and works even faster. To advertise this improvement, our creative team, Ritchie and Charlie, has come up with the idea of setting up a demonstration in a supermarket and challenging shoppers to test their own multi-surface spray cleaners against Cleen-Up.

THE COPY MEETING

The agency—in the persons of Ritchie, Charlie, and Sandra—presents its hidden-camera concept to Jack, the brand manager, in exactly the same way as they presented the "Helping Hand" commercial: in a copy meeting. Of course since the project hasn't been filmed yet, Ritchie and Charlie don't have a script or an accurate storyboard to present. Instead, they talk Jack through the concept in general terms and indicate the flow they hope to see in the final commercial:

Charlie: "We see the commerical opening on a close-up of two grease stains on a countertop. The voice-over announcer will give the challenge, 'Is your multi-surface cleaner faster than Cleen-Up? Mrs. Smith thinks so.' Then we'll cut to a shot of Mrs. Smith to have her tell us how great she thinks her product is. The interviewer will then show her the grease and ask her to clean one stain with her product and the other with New Cleen-Up. While she is still scrubbing the surfaces, he will ask her how each product is doing and which she thinks is doing a faster job of removing the stain. We'll end each interview by asking the woman, 'Which multi-surface cleaner will you buy next time?' To which we hope she'll reply, 'Cleen-Up.' "

Jack: "Why are you suggesting we start on the grease stains?"

Charlie: "We want to set up the cleaning demonstration."

Jack: "But you don't mention the grease or even cleaning at that point."

Ritchie: "We do ask, 'Is your cleaner faster than Cleen-Up?' Don't you think that implies cleaning, Jack?"

Jack: "Maybe—but it isn't as clear as I'd like it to be."

Charlie: "We could start on the woman as she is talking to the interviewer—that is, while the voice-over announcer is challenging the viewer, we could see Mrs. Smith talking with the interviewer, which would begin to give us some feeling about her. That way she doesn't come out of left field when she starts talking about how good she thinks her product is."

Jack: "That might work. I like the idea of testimonials for this product because it is a chance to get consumers actually involved in using the product. The earlier we see the woman, the better we can get to know her and, hopefully, the more believable she will become. What do you think, Ritchie?"

Ritchie: "I wouldn't see any problem in starting on a wide shot. But maybe then we should change the announcer's copy to something that introduces Mrs. Smith earlier. Something like, 'Mrs. Smith thinks her spray cleaner is pretty good.' Then we cut right to Mrs. Smith saying how great she thinks her brand is."

Jack: "Good! I like that. Now how do you plan to shoot this concept?"

Ritchie: "We've been working with JoAnne, and we think we can make it work by hiding two cameras. One will be used for wide shots of the women talking to the interviewer, and the other will get close-up shots of them as well as of the stains for the cleaning demonstration."

Jack: "How much do you estimate this project will cost?"

Sandra: "We figure about a hundred and twenty-five thousand, which includes one day of filming."

Jack: "For one day of filming!"

Ritchie: "Yes, but we plan to interview twenty women during the day and, out of those, hope to get ten we can use. If this holds true, the cost of the production will be amortized over all ten commercials, which means that each one will cost only twelve thousand five hundred. That's much less than the cost for one thirty-second 'Helping Hand' commercial."

Jack: "Do we need ten commercials for this campaign, Sandra?"

Sandra: "If this project goes as we expect it to, we will have enough advertising for the whole year."

Jack: "Will these all be thirty-second commercials?"

Ritchie: "No, we'd use a combination of sixty- and thirty-second ones."

Jack: "I see. But how can we be sure that the women will say the right things?"

Ritchie: "We can never be sure that they all will. But to help point them in the right direction we've prepared a guide for the interviewer that will help him understand the flow we're looking for in the interview."

THE INTERVIEWER

The interviewer is a key member of the hidden-camera team. He can be a professional interviewer or an actor whose specialty is this kind of interviewing. He is the one who talks to the women; walks them through the demonstration, if there is one; and asks their opinion of the product. The interviewer becomes the director of the interview, probing the women with questions that, it is hoped, will get answers that can be cut together to make a commercial.

An interviewer for a hidden-camera commercial must be very sensitive to people. He must be able to make them feel relaxed and willing to talk to him, open up to him, so he can get more than one-word answers to his questions. He must also fully understand the product and the objectives of the specific project he is working on, and know what the final advertising is supposed to look like so he can ask the right questions.

The guide that the agency creative team prepares for the interviewer becomes like his script. It has sample questions for him to ask and indicates points of special interest that should be probed. Most of the interviewer's questions will be cut out of the final commercial because they aren't important to the advertising. However, when a question is important and will be used, the guide will indicate this and give the interviewer the exact wording to use.

The following could be the interview guide for the New Cleen-Up project:

Cleen-Up Interview Guide

1. What multi-purpose spray cleaner do you use?
2. Do you think your cleaner is fast? Why? How long have you been using it? (Probe for how well she likes her brand.)

3. EXACT WORDING—What would you say if I told you there was something faster than your brand? (Probe for skepticism.)
4. EXACT WORDING—This is kitchen grease we have built up. We'd like you to clean one stain with your brand and the other with New Cleen-Up. (Probe during demonstration for reactions to cleaning.)
5. What brand will you buy next time? Why? (Probe for good comments about Cleen-Up.)

PRODUCTION

There are several differences between hidden-camera production and producing a commercial like "Helping Hand." For example, in "Helping Hand" it was very important to build the right set, one that would create the proper environment for the actors in the commercial. In hidden-camera production it is much more important to figure out a way to hide the equipment and crew so that they are totally invisible to the casual observer.

Further, it isn't necessary in a hidden-camera production to cast actors who can deliver dialogue in a convincing manner. What is needed is an interviewer who has the ability to make women shoppers comfortable enough to give good testimony.

As far as a director for a hidden-camera project is concerned, he doesn't have to be a specialist in the use of a camera or have the ability to work well with actors and get them to deliver their dialogue in a natural way. What is important is that the director be good with logistics, because hidden-camera production involves several problems: Where are the cameras going to be hidden? How will the agency creative/production team be able to see what is going on during the interview? How can you communicate with the interviewer without alerting the woman being interviewed? What is the best way to set up the demonstration before each interview? How should women shoppers be recruited for the interview? All these questions must be resolved long before the shooting day, so the director must be an expert at this kind of problem-solving.

Andy, the man chosen to direct the New Cleen-Up project, has been directing hidden-camera testimonial commercials for twenty years. After talking to the agency creative/production team, he decides that the best setup for this project would be near the back of a large supermarket in which the aisles are fairly wide. This area will provide him with several places to hide his cameras—for example, behind the glass of the meat counter or in the back storage area, where he can shoot through the windows on the swinging doors.

To allow the agency team to see what is going on during the interview, Andy will use special-film cameras with a small television camera attached. The TV camera will be hooked up to a monitor in a corner of the back room where the agency people can sit to see exactly what is being shot.

The problem of communication with the interviewer is solved by a wireless earphone, much like the ones used on television news programs. The earphone will be almost invisible on the interviewer and will be tuned to a microphone in the back room. This will enable the director to talk with the interviewer without interrupting the interview.

Andy makes sure that there is enough time in the schedule to permit the changing of countertops from interview to interview. He also arranges for several countertops to be available so that while one is being used for an interview, another can be gotten ready for the next interview.

Since the New Cleen-Up project depends on recruiting women shoppers in a supermarket and asking them to help in a research project for a new spray cleaner, production assistants are sent into the store to talk to shoppers. Their job is to find women who can express themselves well, because the success of the project depends on finding women who are articulate and able to state their opinions clearly. When a candidate is found, she is asked if she would like to participate. She is told that she will receive ten dollars for her time and that the interview will take approximately ten minutes.

If the woman agrees to take part in the project, she is taken to the special area that has been set up in the back of the market for the interview, where all she sees is a countertop, with two grease stains on it, and a display of all the spray cleaners sold in the market. What she doesn't see are the two cameras and microphones hidden in the area to record the interview. As mentioned previously it is important—both creatively and legally—that the woman not know that she is being recorded until after the interview.

Let's assume that Mrs. Smith is a shopper who has agreed to participate in a research interview. In the special area, she is introduced to Rob, the interviewer, who spends several minutes getting to know her. He asks questions about her family, where she comes from, what kinds of foods she likes to cook—all for the purpose of putting her at ease and getting her used to answering his questions. When Rob thinks the time is right, he gives an agreed-upon cue (an unobtrusive action—a cough or a specific question) which tells the director that he is ready to start the actual interview.

The cameras are rolled and the interview begins. Camera 1 has a shot of Rob and Mrs. Smith behind the counter, and camera 2 has a close-up of Mrs. Smith alone.

Rob: "Mrs. Smith, do you use one of these multi-surface spray cleaners?"

Mrs. Smith: "Yes, this one."

Rob: "How long have you been using it?"

Mrs. Smith: "Ever since it came out—about ten years or so, I guess."

Rob: "I guess you like it then."

Mrs. Smith: "Yes."

Rob: "Why?"

Mrs. Smith: "Well, it cleans good—you know, fingerprints off the walls, grease off the stove, things like that."

Rob: "Do you think your cleaner is fast?"

Mrs. Smith: "Sure do! You just spray and—zip!—you can clean the dirt right off."

Rob: "What would you say if I told you that there was something faster than your brand?"

Mrs. Smith: "Well, I've tried a couple of other brands, and they just don't work as well. So I always come back to my good old standby."

Rob: "So you don't think there could be anything faster?"

Mrs. Smith: "Oh, I don't know. I guess there could be something faster, but I'd have to see it to believe it."

Rob: "Well, Mrs. Smith, that's why we're here. To see if New Cleen-Up can beat your spray cleaner. Are you ready for the test?"

Mrs. Smith: "I guess so."

Rob shows Mrs. Smith the grease stains on the countertop as camera 2 moves to show a close-up of the grease. Camera 1 still has a shot of Rob and Mrs. Smith behind the counter.

Rob: "This is kitchen grease we have built up. We'd like you to clean one stain with your brand and the other with New Cleen-Up."

Mrs. Smith sprays the stain on the right with her cleaner and rubs several times to get the countertop clean.

Rob: "How's it working, Mrs. Smith?"

Mrs. Smith: "Great—just like always."

Rob: "Okay. Now clean the other stain with New Cleen-Up."

She sprays New Cleen-Up on the other stain and wipes the grease off the countertop immediately.

Mrs. Smith: "That's amazing!"

Camera 1 tightens up a little to get a closer shot of Rob and Mrs. Smith. Camera 2 moves back to a close-up shot of Mrs. Smith alone.

Rob: "What did you say?"

Mrs. Smith: "I said, that's amazing! This Cleen-Up cut through that grease so fast!"

Rob: "But what happened to your brand?"

Mrs. Smith: "My brand didn't work as fast. Now that's really something!"

Rob: "Mrs. Smith, read the New Cleen-Up label. What does it say?"

Mrs. Smith: " 'New Cleen-Up with improved grease-cutting action.' Well, it really works."

Rob: "How do you know?"

Mrs. Smith: "I just did it. This New Cleen-Up really works and I know, because I just did it."

Rob: "Did what?"

Mrs. Smith: "Cleaned up that yucky stain. Cleen-Up just cleaned it right up!"

Rob: "But your brand—"

Mrs. Smith: "My brand just didn't clean as fast."

Rob: "Mrs. Smith, let me ask you one more question. What brand will you buy next time?"

Mrs. Smith: "No doubt about it. If it works that well at home, I'll have to buy New Cleen-Up from now on."

Rob: "You don't have to say that just to make me happy."

Mrs. Smith: "No, I mean it. It really works. You saw it yourself."

Rob: "Well, that's it. Thank you, Mrs. Smith."

The interview is over, and now Mrs. Smith is in for a surprise. Harry, the production assistant, takes her into the manager's office and gives her the ten dollars that was promised. Then he tells her that the interview was filmed. At first, she thinks he's joking, because she hadn't seen any cameras. But when it's explained to her that the cameras were hidden, she is finally convinced and signs an affidavit stating that she had no idea that the interview was being filmed when she gave her testimony, that she spoke her own thoughts, and that nobody prompted or prejudiced her thinking. She is next told that her interview may be among those chosen to be made into television advertising, and is asked to sign a release giving the advertising agency and the makers of New Cleen-Up the right to use her name, picture, and testimony in any advertising for the product, if they choose to do so.

Mrs. Smith: "What happens if you do decide to make a commercial out of my interview?"

Harry: "We will contact you and ask you to sign a Screen Actors Guild contract. This will protect you and guarantee that you get paid just as though you were a professional actor."

Mrs. Smith: "What does that mean?"

Harry: "The advertising agency has a contract with the Screen Actors' Guild and agrees to pay performers a standard fee for their services. You'd get at least two hundred and seventy-five dollars. You might get as much as several thousand dollars, though, depending on how the commercial is used and where it is shown."

Mrs. Smith: "Wow!"

Harry: "Now, Mrs. Smith, we'd like to ask you not to tell any of your friends about what has happened here until this evening. That will give us time to finish our work here without causing a lot of excitement."

THE TRANSCRIPT

Once the shooting day is finished, the sound track is sent out to have transcripts made of all the interviews. These transcripts, containing everything said during the filmings, are returned to the agency, and the creative team goes through them very carefully. Each interview is graded in terms of content. The best are pulled out and Ritchie and Charlie begin to "write" their commercial. Actually, what they do is edit the interviews on paper, adhering to the following simple, but rigid, guidelines:

1. *No comment or statement may be taken out of order.* This means that the interview must be edited so that the comments made in the commercial appear in the same order that

they were given in the interview. For example, near the end of her interview, Mrs. Smith had said, "Cleen-Up just cleaned it right up." Later she'd said, "Cleen-Up really works. You saw it yourself." If Ritchie and Charlie want to use these statements in the advertising, they have to use them in precisely that order. They can't have Mrs. Smith saying, "Cleen-Up really works. You saw it yourself. Cleen-Up just cleaned it right up."

2. *Comments or statements may not be taken out of context.* This means that a word or two cannot be taken from several different comments to create a new statement. Whenever possible, an entire statement should be used. Also, a statement from one part of the interview may not be used to answer a question from another part.

3. *No answer to a leading question may be used without using the question itself.* A "leading question" is one calculated to put an idea into the respondent's mind. For example, "Wouldn't you say New Cleen-Up is a great product?" is a leading question; it plants the thought that New Cleen-Up is indeed just that.

4. *The final commercial must reflect the true feelings and experience of the woman interviewed.* This means that statements cannot be taken out of context to create the impression that a woman loved the product when, in fact, she didn't.

The interviews in the New Cleen-Up project can be divided into five categories: (1) comments about how good the woman thinks her brand is; (2) the challenge and the woman's reaction to it; (3) the actual demonstration; (4) the woman's positive reaction to New Cleen-Up; and, (5) her statements about using New Cleen-Up in the future. To Ritchie and Charlie, picking the best comments from each category in an interview is like picking the best takes from each scene in the "Helping Hand."

Mrs. Smith's interview is the first one that the team works on. After selecting her best comments, they put them together to see if they make sense. If the selection works, it gives them some idea of what the final commercial will look like. But they still haven't come up with a sixty-second or thirty-second script; all they have done is identify and organize the best parts of the interview into what seems to be a potentially workable commercial. They won't really know what they have until they actually begin to edit the interview film, for frequently remarks that look good on paper look altogether different on film. There could be a number of reasons for this in the New Cleen-Up interview: Mrs. Smith may have taken too long to make some of her statements; she may not have expressed them with enough enthusiasm; or she may have been looking away from the camera at the wrong time. Until the creative team actually sees a statement combined with the pictures that pertain to it, there's no way of knowing whether or not they will work together for the final commercial. In other words, a hidden-camera commercial can't be written on paper; it must be created in the editing room.

EDITING

Editing a hidden-camera commercial is much like editing any other kind of commercial, except that there is no actual script to follow.

While the creative team is going through the transcripts, Frank, the editor, syncs up the sound track of the interview with the film from camera 1—the camera that had the shot of Rob and Mrs. Smith behind the counter. (The film from camera 2 will be used like the silent-demonstration footage that was shot for the "Helping Hand" commercial and cut in as needed.)

Once camera 1 is in sync with the sound track, Frank begins working on the interview—again, just as he did with the "Helping Hand" commercial—by building a select reel. The difference here is that instead of pulling the selected takes of various scenes, he is pulling selected comments. Once all of Mrs. Smith's good comments are on the reel, Frank and JoAnne are ready to build their hidden-camera testimonial commercial.

JoAnne: "Where do we begin, Frank?"

Frank: "Let's first see if we can cut a sixty-second commercial from this interview. We'll cut one section at a time, then put them all together and see what we've got."

JoAnne: "Okay. Let's start with Mrs. Smith's line, 'Well, it cleans good—you know, fingerprints off the walls, grease off the stove. . . .' "

Frank finds the comment JoAnne wants on the select reel. He backs the film up to make sure there is at least two-and-a-half seconds preceding the statement to allow for the voice-over announcer's opening line, cuts the whole sequence out of the select reel, and begins to build his rough-cut reel.

The second of Mrs. Smith's comments that JoAnne wants to use is: "You just spray and—zip!—you can clean the dirt right off." This remark follows Rob's question, "Do you think your cleaner is fast?" But they don't need the question for the commercial, so Frank cuts it out and edits Mrs. Smith's second comment behind her first one on the rough-cut reel.

Frank now backs up the film to the beginning and runs the whole sequence to see how it works. The film shows Mrs. Smith talking to Rob. She is saying, "Well, it cleans good—you know, fingerprints off the walls, grease off the stove. You just spray and—zip!—you can clean dirt right off." The comments flow together, but there is a problem with the picture: Mrs. Smith appears to jump between her two comments. She doesn't physically move from one side of the screen to the other, but there is a visible jerky movement of her head, and she seems to move a few inches to the left. This is called a "jump cut" and happens any time a sequence is cut out of the middle of a piece of continuous action. In order to eliminate the jump, it is necessary to cut to a totally different shot of the same action. This is where the film from camera 2 comes in.

To create a flow and avoid the jump cut, Frank decides to start with camera 1 for the voice-over announcer. Then, when

Mrs. Smith starts to speak, he cuts to her close-up from camera 2 for her first comment, then back to camera 1 for her second one. Once the scene is cut this way it flows smoothly with no apparent jump from comment to comment.

Next, JoAnne wants to use Rob's question, "What would you say if I told you there was something faster than your brand?" Since this comes right after Mrs. Smith's second comment, Frank extends the shot from camera 1 to include the question, then cuts to the close shot from camera 2 for her answer, "I guess there could be something faster, but I'd have to see it to believe it." Then it's back to the wide shot and camera 1 for the scene showing Rob setting up the demonstration. In this way Frank builds a sixty-second commercial from Mrs. Smith's interview.

New Cleen-Up Mrs. Smith: 60

1. Wide shot	ANNOUNCER: Mrs. Smith thinks her spray cleaner is pretty good.
2. Close-up of Mrs. Smith	MRS. SMITH: Well, it cleans good, you know, fingerprints off the walls, grease off the stove.
3. Wide shot	MRS. SMITH: You just spray and—zip!—you can clean the dirt right off. ROB: What would you say if I told you there was something faster than your brand?
4. Close-up of Mrs. Smith	MRS. SMITH: I guess there could be something faster, but I'd have to see it to believe it.

5. Wide shot

ROB:
This is kitchen grease we have built up. We'd like you to clean one stain with your brand and the other with New Cleen-Up.

6. Close-up as Mrs. Smith uses her brand

ROB:
How's it working, Mrs. Smith?

MRS. SMITH:
Great—just like always.

7. Wide shot as Rob hands her New Cleen-Up.

ROB:
Okay. Now clean the other stain with New Cleen-Up.

8. Close-up as she uses New Cleen-Up

MRS. SMITH:
That's amazing!

9. Wide shot

MRS. SMITH:
Cleen-Up cut through that grease so fast!

ROB:
But what happened to your brand?

MRS. SMITH:
My brand didn't work as fast. Now that's really something!

ROB:
Read the New Cleen-Up label. What does it say?

10. Close-up of Mrs. Smith reading label

MRS. SMITH:
New Cleen-Up with improved grease-cutting action. Well, it really works.

11. Wide shot

MRS. SMITH:
This New Cleen-Up really works and I know, because I just did it.

ROB:
Did what?

MRS. SMITH:
Cleaned up that yucky stain.
Cleen-Up just cleaned it right up!

12. Close-up of Mrs. Smith   MRS. SMITH:
No doubt about it. If it works that
well at home, I'll have to buy
New Cleen-Up from now on.

When they are satisfied with the sixty-second commercial, Frank and JoAnne concentrate on getting a thirty-second one from the same interview. This is called a "lift."

Frank: "We can't use both of Mrs. Smith's opening comments in the thirty-second version."

JoAnne: "I know. Her first statement is about more uses for her brand."

Frank: "But her second comment is faster and that's very important when you are dealing with thirty seconds."

JoAnne: "What would that do to our flow?"

Frank: "In the sixty-second commercial we're using the wide shot for Mrs. Smith's second comment and Rob's following question. We could start this one with the wide shot, keep it through Rob's question, then cut to the close-up for Mrs. Smith's line, 'I'd have to see it to believe it.' "

JoAnne: "Let's try it."

Sometimes no amount of hard work will make it possible to lift a thirty-second testimonial from a sixty-second one. Perhaps the demonstration takes too long or the comments needed just won't work together in the time allotted. But our team is lucky, and eventually they are able to lift a thirty-second commercial from Mrs. Smith's interview.

1. Wide shot

ANNOUNCER:
Mrs. Smith thinks her spray cleaner is pretty good.

MRS. SMITH:
You just spray and—zip!—you can clean the dirt right off.

ROB:
What would you say if I told you there was something faster than your brand?

2. Close-up of Mrs. Smith

MRS. SMITH:
I'd have to see it to believe it.

3. Wide shot

ROB:
This is kitchen grease we have built up. We'd like you to clean one stain with your brand and the other with New Cleen-Up.

4. Close-up as Mrs. Smith uses her brand

ROB:
How's it working, Mrs. Smith?

MRS. SMITH:
Great—just like always.

ROB:
Okay. Now clean the other stain with New Cleen-Up.

5. Wide shot as Rob hands her New Cleen-Up

6. Close-up as she uses New Cleen-Up

MRS. SMITH:
That's amazing!

7. Wide shot as she reads the label

MRS. SMITH:
New Cleen-Up with improved grease-cutting action.

8. Close-up of Mrs. Smith

MRS. SMITH:
If it works that well at home, I'll have to buy New Cleen-Up from now on.

Once the Mrs. Smith commercials are edited into rough-cut form, the creative team joins JoAnne to screen them at Frank's office. Frank threads up the sixty-second version first:

Ritchie: "That's really good. It works very well with the demo, don't you think so, Charlie?"

Charlie: "Yes, we've got good testimony about the product, a good demo, and Mrs. Smith comes off very relaxed and believable."

Frank: "We were also able to lift a thirty-second version."

Ritchie: "Let's see it."

Frank puts up the thirty-second rough cut.

Ritchie: "Not bad. The demo is very strong in this version. What do you think, Charlie?"

Charlie: "I agree that the demo works well in the thirty, but I miss a lot of Mrs. Smith's personality. In the sixty we get a chance to know her because of her longer answers; in the thirty, she doesn't come off as natural."

JoAnne: "We need both sixties and thirties, don't we?"

Charlie: "Yes, we do. Are there any other interviews that might work in a thirty?"

JoAnne: "Mrs. Jones's will. But I don't think we can get a good sixty out of hers, because all her comments are very short."

Charlie: "Okay, let's do this. We'll take the sixty and thirty of Mrs. Smith back to the agency, and show it to management and the account group to get their input and make sure we're on the right track. If they think the thirty works, we'll present it to the client with the sixty. If they don't think it works, we'll come back and work on a thirty from Mrs. Jones."

At the agency, the creative management liked what they saw. They agreed with Charlie that the sixty-second version was a good commercial and that Mrs. Smith was slightly more natural in that one than in the thirty. But they also shared Ritchie's opinion that the strong demo in the thirty made it a good piece of advertising too.

The account group also liked both versions; they therefore screened them for Jack.

Jack agreed that the Mrs. Smith commercials were promising ones with which to start the New Cleen-Up advertising campaign. He recognized the slight weakness in the shorter version, but nevertheless felt that, together, the thirty and sixty made a good pair. Having decided this, he approached his management and was able to get their prompt authorization to air both commercials in the market where New Cleen-Up was to be introduced.

Now that client approval has been given, the two testimonial commercials follow the same path as did "Helping Hand." The sound tracks are equalized and mixed; the picture is made into optical negatives, which in this case is very easy because there are no complicated opticals; and soon the Mrs. Smith commercials are on the air introducing New Cleen-Up with "improved grease-cutting action."

16. *The Real People*

The people you met in the story about Cleen-Up weren't
real in themselves, but they represented actual people with different job functions and showed how they work together. The
characters allowed us to dramatize the process of advertising and
production. However, the advertising/production industry is
more than a process; it is real people engaged in real jobs, and
one of the questions most often asked of those in the industry is,
"How do I get one of those jobs?"

Entrance into the marketing side of advertising is fairly
straightforward. Many large advertising agencies and consumer
goods corporations have training programs for young account
executives or brand managers. The prospect is hired right out of
college and put to work learning the "real world" of marketing.
If he learns well, he is gradually moved up the respective cor-
porate ladder until he or she is a full account executive or brand
manager.

On the other hand, there is no formula or direct route into
the creative or technical world of advertising and production.
Breaking in takes a combination of talent, desire, connections,
perseverance, and luck. Having said this, we'll let some of the
people we interviewed for the book tell you in their own words

how they got into the business. What follows are excerpts of interviews with a cross section of the people we talked to.

Lloyd Fink   *Associate Creative Director*

"It was 1969 and I was doing graduate work in English. At that time I had an apartment in the Bronx that was costing me sixty-five dollars a month, and I found myself at a point where I couldn't pay the rent and needed a job. A couple of days before, I had run into a guy at a party who was a creative director. Now I didn't even know what a creative director did, but I knew it had something to do with being creative, and I was creative; so I called him up and told him that I was looking for a job. He asked me what I did and I said, 'I wrote for the school literary magazine and I'm into photography.' He said, 'Why don't you come up to the agency tomorrow, bring your work, and have a look around.'

"The next day I went to the agency with my photographs and my writing from the literary magazine. He looked at both and was very diplomatic. He said, 'I don't think you should be in photography.' I said, 'Well, what about being a writer?' He told me that advertising required a different kind of writing than I had been doing and to take a look around and see. I did and thought, 'Hey, this is nice. I'd like to pursue this a little.'

"I hung around there for about two months. This guy gave me fictitious assignments to help me learn how to write advertising; he even had one of his art directors help me put together a spec book. Then, instead of a résumé I wrote a short story about myself and went out knocking on doors.

"At Doyle-Dane they said, 'No.' I went to Wells, Rich, and Green, fought my way past the secretaries and they said, 'No.' I was getting very despondent; I was nothing for two. Then a Madison Avenue bus passed me with a poster on it that said, 'We're looking for the best $12,000 copywriter in the business.' I ran to the nearest phone booth, put in a dime, called them up and said, 'I don't know who the best twelve-thousand-dollar copywriter is, but I know who the best nine-thousand-dollar copywriter is.' They said, 'Oh, yeah? Come on up.'

"I went right over. It was a small agency—Calderhead/Jackson. We talked for a while, I showed them my book and short story, and went home. They called me the next day and offered me the job at eight thousand. I was a pretty nervy kid in those days and told them it had to be nine thousand or nothing, and you know what? They hired me at nine thousand.

"About four months after I was hired I was working late one night with the guy who hired me. He asked me if I knew why they had hired me. I said, 'My book?' He said, 'No, your book stunk. But your short story was fabulous. We knew you could write.'

"And that's the story."

Paul Fisher *Editor*

"When I was about sixteen years old, back in the late 1950s, I decided that I would have to supplement the family income. So my mother and I went down to the local drive-in movie and I applied for a job as a car parker. The next year I was working in the snack bar; and a year after that I was managing the place. At that point I made a deal with the boss: If I could run his percentage higher than what it had been, by keeping the place open later in the year, I would take a percentage of what was over and above the norm. In order to keep the place open later in the year, I had to run the projectors myself, and at that point I got into the projectionists' union.

"Then I was drafted, and after a great deal of rigmarole, ended up in Queens at the Army Pictorial Center. I was sent there to run projectors; but I was military, and the guys who ran the projectors were civilian union guys who didn't want the military taking over their jobs. To avoid trouble I was stuck in the editing room as an apprentice, with a fellow named Nick Myers.

"Nick's dad was a pretty big editor in the television industry.

He and Nick had worked on shows like *East Side, West Side*—
things like that. Anyway, Nick had gotten drafted and there we
were together in the editing room at the Army Pictorial Center.

"They gave us a training film to edit. Now, a training film
or a medical film usually took up to two months to finish; but
we turned that first film around in less than a week. We did a
lot of training films after that, forty-two, all told—Vietnam staff
reports and things like that.

"Thinking back on it, being drafted was one of the best
things that ever happened to me. Between the army and Nick, I
learned my craft and here I am today."

John McShane   *Commercial Director*

"I went to school at Northwestern University near Chicago
and wanted to be either an actor or a director. I guess I really
wanted to direct live television; that's what I liked best out of all
the courses there.

"When I graduated from Northwestern, I went right into the
service, and when I got out, I hit the streets looking for a job.
That was in 1958, the end of '58, and there was a slight reces-
sion going on. It was slight enough so that there weren't many
jobs in Chicago.

"I went to all the network stations and that was really a joke.
There was no way of getting a job as a director for a network or
even a local kind of show. Then I went to the advertising agencies and tried to become a producer. That didn't work out either
and I had some heavy-weight people pushing for me. I even
talked to Dick Foote of Foote, Cone and Belding and he was
very helpful and solicitous, but no job. So I ended up at CBS
Radio filling out the announcer's log—a glorified file clerk. I
was making fifty-eight dollars a week and had to commute from
Waukegan. All in all, it was not a very satisfying sort of life; but
I was working.

"Then one Sunday night I ran into a college classmate in a
saloon in Chicago and he told me that they were interviewing

for an assistant director at this film company. The next morning at eight-thirty sharp, I was at Fred Niles Production at twenty-two West Hubbard. I told them I wanted to interview for the job of assistant director and got to talk with the production manager. Then I had an interview with Lloyd Bathune, the director who was looking for the assistant. I guess they liked what they saw because they hired me.

"At that time I was completely, totally, one-hundred-percent ignorant of moviemaking. I had never seen a motion picture camera, never been in a motion picture studio. I didn't even know that they made films in Chicago, which I found very hard to believe, having gone to school at Northwestern. But that job was so exciting that I couldn't do anything but make movies.

"Two months after I got the job I moved into Chicago to be closer to the studio. I worked as many hours as Lloyd thought was necessary, even Saturdays and Sundays. It was like a postgraduate course completely devoted to making films.

"What I got working with Lloyd was really on-the-job training. When I started, everything was brand new to me—everything. It was like an absolutely brand new world. But I had a foot in the door. I was in the ultimate position to learn, because the production company was totally self-sufficient. They had their own prop room, their own sound room, their own editorial department. Every possible means of learning film was under one roof and you could do it all—professionally.

"I worked with Lloyd for fifteen months and that's where I learned film—learned to be a director. Of course the more refined parts of filmmaking and the discipline of working with actors come only with experience, but I learned the basics— every phase of making movies—all from that first job."

Elaine Morris *Agency Producer*

"I was a sophomore in college and thought that I might want to make advertising my career. So I got into a summer program at Doyle-Dane-Bernbach, where they hired college students as 'floaters.' What you did was float around the agency during the summer, filling in as a typist wherever you were needed. That job was terrific for me because I got to see almost all the departments of the agency, which helped solidify for me that I wanted to get into the advertising field. The next summer I was one of only ten students asked to come back, which I did, and I floated again.

"Oddly enough, though, I didn't work in the production department either of those summers. It was only when I came back the following Christmas that I was asked to work in production. I was on vacation and had come back to visit the friends I'd made in the agency. In the personnel department, they asked me if I would work that week in production, where the secretary to the head of production was out. I hemmed and hawed and finally said that I would, and that's how I got my foot in the door in the production department.

"I hit it off right away with the head of production, and when his secretary left in the spring to open a pottery shop, he called me at school and asked if I would be his secretary when I graduated. Now I didn't picture myself as a secretary for the rest of my career, but I figured it was a great first step.

"When I got there after graduation, however, the personnel officer who hired me said very plainly from across her desk, 'If you are hired here as a secretary, that is all you will ever be here. This is not a training ground for students or anybody else. If we hire you here to type, all you will ever do is type. Do not expect that we will offer you another job or promote you or train you to do anything else.' I said, 'Fine,' and thought I'd make my own way.

"My boss also told me that they didn't promote secretaries; but I was very persistent. I wouldn't let up on the poor guy. As far as I was concerned, there was a job in production for me and I knew I could do it. I bugged him for over a year and he finally said to me, 'I can't promote you because we don't promote secretaries.' I said, 'Fine, so fire me and hire me as something else.' Well, he didn't fire me, but he did eventually promote me to an assistant radio producer, which started the resurgence of a training program in the department.''

Suzanne Parcarzi *Editor*

"I studied film in college and wanted to be an editor for as long as I knew that I wanted to be in the film business. When I graduated, I took the New York Yellow Pages and looked up every editing place in town. Then, résumé in hand, I started knocking on doors, and hit about seventy places before I got lucky.

"What happened was, I walked into this place and they said that they needed a messenger and someone who could also do a little bookkeeping. The catch was they were looking for a girl because they wanted her to answer the phone when the receptionist went to lunch. Well, I knew a little about bookkeeping, and I'm the right sex, so I got the job.

"Once I was in, it was fairly easy to make myself useful. Since I knew things about editing, they asked me to help out when they got really busy—you know, doing things like syncing up the dailies. Anyway, I worked hard, and as people left the company, they never hired someone new. Instead, they just moved me up and eventually I became a full editor.''

Stuart Raffel *Assistant Producer*

"I graduated from Ohio University with a degree in radio and TV production. When I got out of school I had two options: I could either go the small-station route and work my way through Ohio and maybe to a decent-size market, and from there possibly on to New York; or I could come straight to New York and give it a shot. I figured the worst I could lose if I came straight to New York was a year's time, and at age twenty-two, that seemed like a good gamble.

"However, I didn't come straight to New York from college. On the advice of a friend, I stayed in Cincinnati and worked to build up a nest egg. I got a job as a waiter, and when I thought I had enough money to last me three or four months, I came East.

"When I got here, I was willing to take any sort of production job, whether it was at a tape-facility or film-production company or an advertising agency—anywhere, just to get my first job and meet people and continue to learn and broaden my horizons.

"Well, my money didn't last me two months, but I got lucky. Someone I had just met and my friend in Cincinnati both called the head of production of this agency on the same day and suggested that I might be someone that he would want to interview. I guess the fact that both these guys called him on the same day impressed him, because he called me and asked me to come in for an interview.

"I went to see him the next day. He interviewed me and I was offered a job in their in-house production facility, which is used as a training ground for young producers. What we did in the in-house production unit was provide a service to the different groups in the agency. If someone needed to videotape a casting session or transfer a film to three-quarter-inch videocassette, we could do it in the in-house facility and save the expense and time of going out of the agency to get the work done. Working in the facility gave me an overall feel for the agency. I dealt with people from every department: from casting and production to account people and traffic—everybody used our services.

"You know, they don't promise you anything when you get hired into the in-house production unit. But if you do a good job and they like the way you get along with people, you have a good chance of being promoted to assistant producer, and from there you're on your way."

Ellen Ribner *Agency Producer*

"I think my story begins when I was a high school history
and economics teacher. I realized one day that I was getting an
intellectual kick putting the pieces together, not in the teaching
itself. I decided that maybe the best way to use my background
and knowledge was not to teach, but to work in documentary
films and television in some way. I quit my teaching job and
tried to get into film work.

"Well, that was back in 1968 when I think every other
young person in the world wanted to be in film and television.
And since I had no pull and absolutely no direction or training
in the field, I just walked the sidewalks looking for a job in
production. I did that for two months and became totally frus-
trated. I went to every television station, every radio station, and
every other place I could think of in the city of New York, and I
couldn't get a job. Then I saw an ad in the *New York Times* for
a production assistant. I called the number and went to a place
called MPO Videotronics, where I met with a director of television commercials named Michael Cimino.

"I was the first person Michael interviewed. I can still remember what he was wearing: thongs, white dungarees, an
alligator shirt and sunglasses; and he informed me that I was the
first of about forty people he was sure he would be seeing. He
didn't interview me, really, just had me talk about myself for
about forty minutes; then I left and thought nothing in the
world would ever come of it. But four days later I got a phone
call that I had the job and was to report to work the next day.

"When I started working for Mike, I had absolutely no idea
what to expect. I didn't even know what a production assistant
did, but I soon found out. I started at the bottom as a go-fer,
and it was very tough and very difficult and required a great deal
of adjustment. You come out of college and graduate school
thinking you're really something and then you start at the bottom and you're doing dirt; you're doing everything from taking
clothes to the laundry to getting coffee to ordering meals to

hanging up actors' and actresses' clothes in the dressing room. But because I started that way, I really got to learn about film from the bottom up.

"Michael has a great love for film, especially the editing and optical part of it. He took me into sections of MPO—post-opticals, editing, where he spent all of his after-hours. In fact, he hardly ever went home. And I learned about shooting and about photography and about finishing film from him.

"We worked together for the better part of ten years, and during that time he left MPO and left New York to go out to California and devote his time fully to writing screenplays. We worked out an arrangement where I stayed in New York and did the production work that had to be finished on his commercials, and then helped him research his screenplays. We worked on ten screenplays together over those years.

"During that time I also got a job at Westinghouse Broadcasting as the editor for their Documentary Film Department. What we did was take documentaries that they had shot specifically for television, and re-edit them so they could be sold to educational institutions and museums all over the world. That gave me further exposure to editing, which still is one of my favorite parts of television commercials. Anyway, I worked myself up to being production manager and then left to work with Mike on his feature films.

"On *The Deer Hunter*, I lived on location and was in charge of coordinating and securing some of the locations for the American part of that film. I also did a lot of trouble-shooting and dealt with everyone from Jay Rockefeller to the president of National Steel in West Virginia.

"It was a great experience, but when it was over I decided that I didn't want to be on location anymore, didn't want to travel anymore, and didn't want to live in California. So I decided to go back to where I had started in the business—commercials—and called a friend at an advertising agency, where I found out that they had a job for an assistant producer.

"Taking that job was a big decision for me because it meant

starting at the bottom again, and taking an enormous salary cut to boot. But, thinking it through, I felt it was the best thing for me, so I did it. I started my third career by becoming an assistant producer, and then an associate producer, and about a year after that, finally, at the ripe old age of thirty-three, a full producer."

GLOSSARY

Account Executive   The person responsible for handling an account within an advertising agency. He is the major contact with the client.

Account Management   One of the departments in an advertising agency. This group consists of the account executives, their assistants, and their supervisors.

Action   1. The command given by the director to start a scene. 2. Any business or movement by the players within a scene.

Animation   1. *Film term:* Drawings that are photographed in sequence, one frame at a time, to give the illusion of motion. 2. *Acting term:* The quality that gives life to a performance, that makes it lively, that contributes to playing a scene with more vigor.

Announcer Track   A sound track of the announcer's voice. This track is usually recorded after the commercial is filmed.

Answer Print   A print of the finished commercial in which the picture and sound track are put together for the first time. *See also* Composite Print.

Aperture   1. The iris in a camera lens that allows light to pass through. 2. The square opening in a camera that frames the picture.

Apple Box   A sturdy square wooden box used to elevate people and/or objects on the set.

Art Director   A member of the creative team; draws storyboards;

155

works with writer to develop advertising concepts. He is the visually oriented member of the creative team who works with the producer on the set to create the overall look of the commercial.

Aspect Ratio The standardized relationship of height to width in the television frame, which is 3 to 4.

Assistant Cameraman Crew member; keeps camera in running order during the shooting day. He compiles camera notes that go to the editor and is responsible for sending film to the lab after the shooting day.

Assistant Director (A.D.) Crew member; supervises the crew during the shoot. He also handles business arrangements with suppliers, tradesmen, and whatever civic or police officials are concerned with permits, special cooperation, etc.

Assistant Editor An apprentice film editor who assists a full editor. He is usually responsible for syncing the dailies.

Audio Mix The putting together of two or more sound tracks to make a single master track. It is at the audio mix that the sound is balanced and any special sound effects are added.

Audiotape Magnetic tape, ¼-inch wide, used to record the sound for a commercial.

Available Light Light that exists in the area, and with which a scene is filmed without adding any more; usually, available light is used out-of-doors or in a well-lit room.

Baby 750-watt light.

Baby Legs A tripod with short legs used to get the camera close to the ground.

Backdrop Draping or similar material arranged to serve as an appropriate background for the filming of a scene.

Background The general setting or location in which the action takes place.

Background Light A light used to illuminate the background.

Backlight *See* Rim Light

Barn Doors Adjustable metal flaps that attach to the front of a lighting unit. They are used to focus a light in just the right place.

Beauty Shot A shot in which the product is the hero. This is usually a close-up shot of the product, with no actors.

Bidding The process of asking production companies to estimate the cost of producing a television commercial.

Blimp A soundproof housing around a camera. It muffles the camera noise so that it won't be picked up by the microphones.

Blocking (Staging) The planning of camera positions and the movement of the actors in a scene.

Blow-Up A picture made to appear larger on the screen by an optical process. A blow-up brings the action in a scene closer to the viewer.

Boom *See* Camera Boom; Microphone Boom

Boomman Crew member; holds the mike boom over the actors' heads. He swivels it constantly within the sound range of the actors and well out of vision of the camera.

Bounce Illumination Indirect lighting; an effect achieved by bouncing light off a reflective surface, such as a white card.

Brand Manager (Product Manager) Person responsible for the marketing success of a brand or product. The brand manager is something like the president of his own small company within a large corporation. It is his job to see that the brand grows and stays healthy in the marketplace.

Budget The amount of money a production company has to spend to produce a commercial.

Business A definite bit of action, e.g., pouring a cup of coffee or folding a pile of laundry.

Butterfly An overhead scrim or silk used to soften shadows and to diffuse harsh lighting.

Buy To accept; to approve a specific take.

Callbacks *See* Final Casting

Camera Angle The position of the camera in relation to the subject matter.

Camera Boom A cranelike device on which a camera is mounted. The boom allows extreme freedom of camera movement: up, down, sideways, and in and out.

Camera Equipment (Shooting Equipment) Lenses, film magazines, dollies, etc. Any piece of equipment needed to work directly with the camera.

Camera Lens A shaped, transparent substance, usually glass, attached to the front of the camera. The camera lens focuses light rays on the film being exposed.

Cameraman Crew member; responsible for supervising the lighting of a scene. He also operates the camera, making sure that he is photographing the action exactly as the director wants.

Camera Moves The various positions, in relation to the subject matter, in which the camera is moved while it is running.

Camera Sheet Report filled out by the assistant cameraman. This sheet lists all the information pertinent to the scenes filmed and is very useful in editing the commercial.

Carpenter Crew member; builds the set under the direction of the set designer.

Casting The hiring of actors to fill the roles in a commercial.

Casting Director The person responsible for finding the right talent for a commercial. The casting director is a "matchmaker," bringing together the talent for a commercial and the agency team working on the commercial.

Casting Session The audition where actors read for the parts in a commercial.

Casting Tape Videotape recording of an actor's audition.

Cattle Call 1. A talent audition open to the public. 2. The first casting session for a commercial, to which twenty or more actors are called for each available part; also called "preliminary casting."

Cheat To move or change slightly the position of an object or person in the set to create a new camera angle without moving the camera.

Clapstick A pair of hinged boards that are attached to the top of the slate. The sticks are banged together at the beginning of each sound take, making a visible mark on the film that can be matched to the sound of the clap on the sound track to help the editor synchronize the sound track to the film. *See also* Slate.

Client The person who pays to have the commercial made. *See also* Brand Manager.

Close-up A very close shot of the subject matter. A close-up of an actor, for example, might show only his head and shoulders.

Color Analyzer Equipment used to help set final color in a filmed commercial.

Color Correction Specialized artwork used to make the color of the product package look the same on television as it does in the store.

Commercial Breakdown Analysis of the needs of a commercial in preparation for bidding. In breaking down a commercial, notes are made of the number of scenes to be shot, whether the commercial should be shot on a set or on location, how much time is needed to shoot the commercial, and any special equipment necessary to accomplish the objectives of the project.

Composite Print A film print with both picture and sound track on a single piece of film.

Concept The idea in a commercial.

Conforming Editing the original negative so that it exactly matches the approved rough cut.

Construction The building of the set after plans and design have been approved.

Continuity Scenes occurring in the order provided in the script.

Contrast 1. The difference between the shadows and highlights in lighting a scene. 2. The spread between dark and light areas in a piece of film.

Cookie Material placed in front of a light to cast a patterned shadow on the background.

Copy 1. The advertising. 2. The commercial. 3. The words in a commercial.

Copy Meeting Meeting in which the agency presents advertising to the client.

Copy Strategy A document written jointly by the client and the agency. It includes statements about the purpose of the product, who the advertising should speak to, and what the image of the product and the tone of the advertising should be.

Copy Supervisor A member of an advertising agency's creative management. The copy supervisor may oversee the work of several writers or creative teams.

Crab To move the camera sideways.

Crab Dolly A movable platform that holds the camera. It can be steered in any direction smoothly and silently.

Creative Director The creative head of an advertising agency.

Creative Team Writer and art director who work together to create advertising.

Crew Group of people hired by a production company to do the various jobs necessary to produce a commercial.

Cue Card A card with the talent's lines written on it.

Cue Sheet Prepared by the editor in preparation for mixing the sound track, the cue sheet shows where the special sound effects and music should come in and go out in the track.

Cut 1. *Editorial term:* To edit or shorten a scene by cutting the film; also, to go from one scene to another without opticals. 2. *Production term:* Director's command to stop the action in a scene and turn off the camera and sound-recording equipment.

Cutaway An insert scene used to break away momentarily from the main action in a scene.

Cut Back To return to the main action in a scene.

Cut-in Point Point at which the film editor cuts into a scene to edit it into a commercial.

Cut-out Point Point at which the film editor cuts out of a scene to go to the next scene in a commercial.

Cutter *See* Flag

Dailies (Rushes) The film from the shoot just as it comes from the laboratory. The dailies are screened by the director, cameraman, editor, and agency creative team for the purpose of checking the action, lighting, moves, and general content of the scenes.

Darkroom A lightproof room used for loading and unloading film from magazines.

Definition The sharpness or clearness with which objects are photographed by a lens.

Delivery The way in which a performance is presented; if, for example, an actress reads her lines well, someone might say that he liked the way she "delivered" her lines.

Demonstration The segment of a commercial that shows the viewer how a product works.

Density The degree of darkness or brightness in a film negative.

Depth of Field The range within which objects being photographed are in sharp focus.

Deuce (Junior) A 2,000-watt light.

Developing A laboratory process in which the latent image on the exposed negative is made visible.

Dialogue The words spoken in a commercial.

Diffuser A translucent screen placed in front of a light source to reduce the harshness of the lighting.

Digital Frame Counter Indicator of the number of film frames that have been exposed while filming.

Direction Instruction and guidance given to the talent for their action.

Director The person responsible for overseeing and coordinating all aspects of production. He takes the agency's concept and, with his knowledge, background, and talent, turns it into a piece of advertising. The director plans all the camera moves and interprets the concept for the actors and his crew.

Director's Chair A light and portable wood-framed chair with a slung seat and back, usually of canvas.

Dissolve (Lap Dissolve) A transition from one scene to the next by overlapping the fade-out of the first scene to the fade-in of the next.

Dolly A mobile platform on which the camera is mounted and the cameraman can sit. *See also* Crab Dolly.

Dollying (Tracking) Moving the camera dolly while the camera is filming a scene. *See also* Trucking.

Double Exposure Two separate scenes shot on the same piece of film.

Double System The standard system for shooting filmed commercials. The sound is recorded on an audiotape recorder while the scene is being filmed by the camera. The sound track and film remain separate until joined on the composite print.

Down Shot Shot taken from a high point, looking down.

Downstage The area of the set closest to the camera.

Dressing the Set To decorate a set with the appropriate props.

Dry Run A rehearsal. The actors speak their lines and go through their actions as though the camera were actually filming. The camera may also move just as it would during an actual take.

Dubber A high-quality sound recorder that feeds into a mixing console.

Dubbing The process of recording several sound tracks and mixing them into one composite track.

ECU Extreme close-up.

Edge Numbers Numbers printed on the edge of the original negative. These correspond to numbers on the rough cut and are used to conform the negative to the approved rough cut.

Editing The process of splicing scenes together in a proper order and matching them to the previously recorded sound track.

Editing Rooms Rooms set up to edit commercials.

Editing Tape   Special tape used to join, or splice together, two pieces of film.

Editor   The person who edits the commercial. He also supervises the mixing of the sound track and the creation of the opticals.

Editorial Sync   The lining up of the picture and sound track in an editing machine so that they are directly opposite each other.

Effects   An all-inclusive term for opticals, which includes fades, dissolves, and more complicated opticals such as split-screen effects.

Effects Track   A track with no dialogue, only sound effects and/or music that is to be mixed into the sound track.

Electronic Photography   Videotape.

Equalize   Balance the sound track so that everything is heard at the same level.

Establishing Shot   Wide shot used to orient the viewer to the environment of the scene.

Exposure   The amount of light allowed to pass through the lens. Also, the amount of time the light is allowed to strike the film.

Exposure Meter (Light meter)   A device for measuring the amount of light falling on or being reflected from the subject to be filmed.

Exposure Reading   The lens setting indicated for the light available.

Exterior   Any scene shot out-of-doors.

Extra   A performer best described as part of the background. He/she has no dialogue.

F-Number   F-stop on a camera; any one of the series of markings on the lens barrel that indicate the aperture setting.

Fade   An optical effect in which a scene goes from full light to blackness or vice versa.

Federal Trade Commission   The government bureau charged with policing truth in advertising.

Fill Light   Any light used to minimize shadows in a scene.

Film Magazine   A container for the unexposed film that will be used to shoot a commercial. The film magazine is loaded in a darkroom and then attached to the camera. When all the film in a magazine has been exposed, the film is transferred to cans and the magazine reloaded with unexposed film.

Film Prints   Positive pictures made from the film negative.

Filter   Any number of glass or gelatin devices placed in front of the camera lens to give various effects. Some filters darken the sky, others simulate night conditions. Still other filters are used to balance color values under varying lighting conditions.

Final Approval The decision, after editing is completed, to accept the film without further changes.

Final Casting (Callbacks) The session at which the final decision will be made on which actors to hire.

Fine Cut The rough cut edited to time, with the scenes as they will appear in the final commercial.

Fish Pole A long pole with a microphone suspended from the end. It is hand-held over the acting area. *See also* Microphone Boom.

Flag Any opaque screen used to shade unwanted light off walls. Also used to keep light from hitting directly into the camera lens. Sometimes called a "gobo," "cutter," or "mask."

Flare An undesirable light streak in the processed film.

Flat A painted background supported by a wooden frame. Flats are often used as background for scenes.

Flatbed A machine used in editing.

Focus The point at which a lens produces the sharpest image.

Footage Amount of film shot.

Frame 1. Each individual picture on a strip of motion picture film. 2. Each picture drawn on a storyboard.

Frame-by-Frame Objectives The subject of discussion by the creative team as to how they would like to see each scene shot. Usually takes place at the pre-production meeting.

Framing Composing a shot.

Frequency *Media term:* the number of times a commercial is shown on the air.

Full-Service Company A production company with complete facilities for motion picture production, including editing and opticals.

Gaffer Crew member; electrician who works with the cameraman to light the set.

Gaffer's Tape A wide, very strong adhesive tape used on the set.

Gel, or Gelatin A translucent celluloid-type filter.

Gobo A black screen used to keep unwanted light from entering the camera lens. *See also* Flag.

Go-fer A junior assistant responsible for running errands.

Good Takes Shots that are considered desirable; also called "selected takes."

Grease Pencil   A grease-based pencil used directly on the film by editors to indicate changes or additions. It is easily removed from the film by a soft cloth.

Grip   Crew member; does heavy moving and lifting during the shooting day. Also helps set flags and gobos.

Gross Price   Total cost paid by the client for the production of a commercial. It includes all talent fees, editorial costs, and agency expenses and commission.

Hair Stylist   Crew member; responsible for styling and attending to the talent's hair during the shoot.

Halation   A kickback of reflected light that is shining too strongly into the camera lens.

Hand Model   A model whose hands only are used in a shot. Hand models are often used to perform product demonstrations.

Head   1. Beginning of a scene. 2. Beginning of a commercial.

Head Shot   Close-up shot on an actor's head and shoulders.

High Hat   A mounting device for supporting a camera on something other than a tripod; often used to get the camera close to the ground.

High-key Lighting   The lighting of a scene with few dark tones; most often used to convey a mood of lightheartedness and well-being.

Highlight   The lightest part of a scene or picture.

Hot Spot   1. Any small area in a scene that is too bright. 2. A bad light reflection from a shiny surface.

Image   A photographed likeness exposed on film.

Inky-Dinky   A small 250-watt spotlight.

Insert   A close-up used for explanation.

Inside Propman   Crew member; places props in the set. He is also responsible for the look of the product on the set and often helps set up demonstrations.

Interior   A scene shot inside a building or stage.

Interlock   Sound and picture on separate pieces of film shown together in synchronization.

In the Can   An expression used to indicate that a film has been exposed and put into a metal can.

Into Frame   An expression indicating that something has been placed where the camera can film it.

Iris   Aperture.

Jump Cut The uneven action between two cuts. This occurs when a section of film is removed from a continuous-action scene and the film is respliced.

Junior *See* Deuce

Key Light The main and most intense light used in lighting a scene.

Key Visual The picture of the selling idea in a commercial. For example, if the selling idea is, "A helping hand to clean around the house," the commercial should have several good cleaning shots from different parts of the house; these would be the key visuals.

Lab (Laboratory) The place equipped to develop and print film.

Lap Dissolve *See* Dissolve

Latent Image The invisible picture that has been created in the film emulsion by exposure to light, but which has not yet been made visible by developing.

Lavalier A small microphone hung around an actor's neck.

Leader Blank film at the beginning and end of a commercial used for threading purposes.

Lens *See* Camera Lens

Lens Mount The bracket on the front of the camera that holds the lens.

Lighting The artificial supply of light used on a set for filming.

Lighting a Set The placing of lights in a set to create the desired mood.

Light Meter *See* Exposure Meter

Limbo Word used to signify an absence of background, with the subject being shot in just a pool of light.

Lip Sync The simultaneous filming and dialogue recording of a scene.

Little Black Book The book of names and addresses of crew members compiled by the production manager.

Live Action 1. Action by live actors rather than by animated figures. 2. Action that is taking place at the same time the viewer is watching it.

Location The place, away from the studio, where a commercial is shot. Location shooting is most often done when special backgrounds such as barns, train stations, ski slopes, etc., are needed.

Long Lens A telephoto lens.

Looser Word used to describe a more relaxed performance.

Low-key Lighting The lighting used in a scene to illuminate only the main subjects, with the rest of the set darker and more unobtrusive.

Magazine *See* Film Magazine

Mag Track Any sound track on magnetic tape.

Makeup Person Crew member; applies the actor's makeup for the shoot. During the day he will be standing by on the set to see that the makeup remains exactly as it was at the beginning of the shoot day.

Mask *See* Flag

Master Shot A shot covering all the action of a scene in one continuous take.

MCU (Medium Close-up) A shot that usually frames the actors from the waist up.

Meter Reading The measurement of light with an exposure meter to determine the proper f-stop for the lens.

Microphone A device used for recording sound. It converts sound waves into electric impulses for transmission and recording.

Microphone Boom An adjustable pole that holds the microphone over the actors' heads. *See also* Fish Pole.

Mix The combination of the various sound elements into a single sound track.

Mixer Crew member; operates the tape recorder that records the sound track for a commercial. With the aid of very sophisticated microphones and a mixing machine, he avoids picking up unwanted background sounds and extraneous noise. He also keeps a record of everything recorded.

Mixed Mag The completed 16mm or 35mm magnetic sound track.

Mock-up A specially constructed prop that is built to scale.

Montage The blending together of several different short scenes to create a unified impression.

Mood The viewer reaction generated by the commercial. The mood is created by both the lighting and the way the commercial is performed by the actors.

MOS Shot without sound.

Move In To move the camera closer to the actor during the filming of a scene. Can be accomplished either by pushing the camera closer on a dolly or by using a zoom lens.

Moving Shot A shot made while the camera is in motion.

Moviola A kind of editing machine that allows the playing of the sound track in sync with the picture.

Music Track A track with the music for a commercial that will be mixed into the finished sound track.

Nagra A portable audiotape recorder used to record the dialogue on the set.

National Commercial A commercial that will be shown on the networks and all over the country, not just in a small region.

Negative Film that is used to shoot a commercial. When it is developed, the images are reversed—light for dark.

Net Price The production company's estimate of how much it will cost them to produce a commercial. This price does not include talent fees, editorial costs, and agency expenses and commission.

Neutral Density Filter Filter that reduces the amount of light reaching the film in the camera without affecting the color values.

No Seam Word that describes a large roll of heavy paper used for backgrounds; the paper is available in many colors.

One Continuous Take *See* Master Shot

Opening Scene The first scene in a commercial. It always establishes the tone and strives to grab the audience.

Optical Negative Negative of the commercial with all the opticals in it.

Optical, or Step, Printer Machine used to create optical effects.

Opticals Special video effects—dissolves, fades, wipes, etc.

Original Camera Negative Film actually exposed in the camera.

Outside Propman Crew member; hired to work before the shoot day. He gathers the items needed to dress the set or location.

Outtakes Takes of scenes that were shot but not used in the final commercial.

P.A. *See* Production Assistant

Package Clean-Up The removal of the net-weight statement and other extraneous small type from the face of the product package. This is done in television commercials because the small type isn't readable in a commercial except in a very close shot. Cleaning up the package front makes the package look uncluttered and allows the viewer to concentrate on the product's name.

Pan Shot   A shot made while moving the camera in a horizontal arc.

Parity Claims   Claims that establish one product as effective or as valuable as another.

Picture Head   A device on the flatbed editing machine that projects the picture on the film to the television screen at the back of the machine.

Plates   The metal discs, each with a center rod, that are set in a flatbed editing machine. These plates hold the film and sound reels as they are being edited.

Pool of Light   A circle of illumination designed to light a specific object or situation.

Post Scoring   The recording of music and musical sound effects to the film after the commercial has been edited.

Post Syncing   The recording of sound effects and lip sync to edited silent footage.

P.O.V. (Point of View)   Usually a view seen by an actor.

Power Pack   Rechargeable battery built into a portable belt worn by the cameraman and connected to the camera.

Preemptive Claims   Product claims that ignore the existence of all competition; i.e., products that claim that they clean well, are gentle to the skin, or soft to the touch, without any mention of competitive products.

Preliminary Casting   *See* Cattle Call

Pre-production   The period between approval of the advertising concept and the shooting of the commercial. During this time, a director is chosen, actors are cast, sets are built, and all other preparations are made to shoot the commercial.

Pre-production Meeting   Meeting that brings together all the agency, client, and production company people to discuss final details for producing a commercial.

Presence (Room Tone)   The atmosphere of a room in which there is no one talking or moving around.

Print   1. A copy of a commercial. 2. The order given by the director when a take is satisfactory. 3. Any piece of positive film made from a negative.

Producer   The person at the advertising agency responsible for translating the storyboard into film. A producer works with the creative team to bring their idea from a piece of paper to a finished commercial.

Product Claims Claims made in advertising about product performance.

Product Manager *See* Brand Manager

Product Registration The visibility of the product in a commercial.

Product Shots Close-up shots of the product.

Production Assistant (P.A.) Crew member; the production assistant is the go-fer for the production company. Before the shoot, he/she might be used to pick up small props needed for the job. During the shoot, he stands by to run any last-minute errands.

Production Company An independent company hired to produce a commercial. A production company may have several directors and a full crew on staff, or it may consist of only one director, a production manager, and a sales representative.

Production Manager Production company producer. The production manager collaborates with the director and sales representative to develop a budget for a shoot, then works to see that the shoot comes in on budget. He is responsible for hiring all crew members, renting all equipment, and establishing schedules that will bring everything together on the stage the day of the shoot.

Production Schedule The timetable for the production of a commercial.

Projector A machine for projecting film onto a screen.

Props Small items used to decorate a set—e.g., toasters, pictures on the wall, etc.

Pullback The act of moving the camera away from the actor, either by zooming out or moving the dolly back.

Pull-up The second-and-a-half of silent footage at the beginning of every film commercial.

Push In To move the camera closer to the actor, either by zooming in or moving the dolly closer.

Raw Stock Film that has not been exposed or developed.

Reach *Media term:* The number of different people who see a commercial.

Registration *See* Product Registration

Rehearsing Practicing a scene before filming.

Release Prints The final prints of the commercial ready for distribution.

Residual (Re-use Fee) A fee paid to a commercial performer for repeat showings of a commercial. The amount is based on a formula laid out in the Screen Actors' Guild contract with the advertising agencies.

Retake To shoot a scene over again.

Re-use Fee *See* Residual

Rim Light (Backlight) A light that outlines the general shape of the subject. This is accomplished by putting the source of the light behind the subject.

"Roll sound" Command to begin recording sound.

"Rolling" Spoken by the cameraman to tell the director that the camera is on and shooting.

Room Tone *See* Presence

Rough Cut The first edited version of a commercial.

Run-through A pre-filming rehearsal during which the actors go through their parts, and camera moves, if any, are practiced. The run-through is usually timed by the script supervisor to make sure that the scene will play in the time allotted.

Rushes *See* Dailies

Sample Reel A reel of ten to fifteen commercials chosen to represent a director's style and ability. The sample reel is one of the most important tools in selling a director to agency creative teams and producers.

Sandbag A bag filled with sand used on the set as a weight.

Scale The base fee paid to performers or crew members as prescribed by their respective union contracts.

Scene Action taking place at one time in one location.

Scoop A 5,000-watt spotlight.

Scratch Track A rough, temporary recording of the voice-over announcer's lines, usually spoken by the producer. It is used to help edit film that was shot silent and is replaced at the sound mix by a track recorded by a professional announcer.

Screening Room A special room equipped with the machines necessary to screen rough cuts and final prints of commercials.

Scrim A translucent material used to diffuse light. *See also* Butterfly.

Script The written text of a commercial.

Script Clerk *See* Script Supervisor

Script Notes Kept by the script supervisor, they include the time of each take and any comments made about it. The script notes are used in editing a commercial.

Script Supervisor (Script Clerk) Crew member; works closely with the director to ensure that no shots are forgotten during the day. The script supervisor times each scene as it is shot to make sure that it plays in the time allotted and keeps the script notes, which include the time of each take and any comments made about it. It is also the script supervisor's responsibility to make certain that there is continuity from scene to scene.

Segue A dissolve between two sound tracks.

Select Reel A reel of the selected takes put together by the editor. It is from the select reel that the editor will build his rough cut.

Selling Idea A persuasive and memorable encapsulation of the copy strategy. The selling idea sums up the advertising concept in a few well-chosen words. It is the main thought the advertiser wants to leave with the viewers and is often superimposed over a product shot at the end of a commercial.

Session Fee Fee paid to the actors for their work on the shooting day. *See also* Scale.

Set The environment for a commercial constructed on a stage.

Set Designer The person who designs the set.

Set Sketch The drawing of the set made by the set designer.

Setup The placing of the camera and lights in a set position to shoot all or part of a scene. A setup is a measure of time in production because it usually takes between thirty minutes and an hour to change to each new setup.

Shoot 1. The process of exposing film. 2. The commercial filming session.

Shooting Equipment *See* Camera Equipment

Shooting Sequence The order in which a commercial will be shot.

Shot A single piece of film within a scene. *See also* Take.

Shot List A list prepared by the director of the camera shots he wants to take for the commercial.

Signatory A person or company that has a legal contract with a union and therefore the responsibility to adhere to the union rules.

Silent Action The action in a commercial with no dialogue.

Silk A light diffuser. *See also* Butterfly.

Slate A card or blackboard that contains information pertinent to the scene being photographed. It is exposed for several frames immediately before each take to provide the editor with a means of identifying the footage. *See also* Clapsticks.

Slow Motion   An effect that is created by shooting the film at a speed faster than normal and projecting the developed film at normal speed.

Snap Pan   *See* Whip

Soft Focus   Description of an image not in sharp focus.

Soft-Lite   Light source that produces soft or diffused illumination, which minimizes or eliminates shadows.

Sound Console   The audio control board used to mix sound tracks.

Sound Effects   All sound other than dialogue, narration, and music. Sound effects are usually recorded separately and mixed with the dialogue track to create the mixed mag track.

Sound Head   Mechanism that can play back sound from a piece of audiotape.

Sound Stage   A soundproof area created for the production of film or videotape.

Sound Track   1. In production, the magnetic tape that has the sound recorded on it. 2. In the finished print of a commercial, the squiggly white line running down one side of the film.

Sound Transfer   1. The transferring of the ¼-inch audiotape to a 16mm or 35mm mag track. 2. The transferring of the mixed mag track to an optical track.

Soundproof Booth   Separate area in a recording studio where an announcer can read his lines and his microphone won't pick up any outside sound.

Source Lighting   Strong lighting from a single source, such as that coming from a single lamp in a room or sunlight streaming in through a window. This lighting creates heavy shadows on the actors and in the set.

Speed   1. Spoken as a cue to the director that the camera and sound recording equipment are running and in sync. 2. The sensitivity of film to light.

Spider   An eight-wheel dolly designed for filming in confined areas.

Spill   Excess or undesirable light falling on the set or actors.

Splice   The place where two pieces of film are taped together.

Split Screen   A frame optically divided into two or more areas with a different action taking place in each.

Spot 1. A television commercial. 2. A spotlight.

Spotlight A light capable of projecting a focused beam to a specific part of the set.

Spun A gauze light diffuser.

Stage The floor or actual working area in a studio where the filming takes place.

Staging *See* Blocking

Step Printer *See* Optical, or Step, Printer

"Stick it" Command given to clap the clapstick.

Stock Footage Footage from film libraries that is available for use in other films.

Stop Down To reduce the size of the lens aperture.

Stops Numbers on the camera lens that tell how much light is coming in through the aperture. The lens can be set by these numbers to help control the amount of exposure for each shot.

Storyboard A series of pictures drawn by the art director to show the proposed flow of an advertising concept. The storyboard places the words and pictures of a concept in relation to each other for the first time.

Strike To take down the set.

Superiority Claims Claims that establish one product as the best in its category.

Swish Pan The panning of the camera from one side to the other while it is running to produce a blurring effect.

Sync The perfect synchronization of picture and sound track.

Sync Motor Motor that drives the separate picture and sound tracks at the same speed so that they stay in sync.

Take The filming of a scene from the time the clapsticks are clapped until the time the camera is cut.

Talent An actor or actress performing in a commercial.

Teamster Crew member; drives the equipment truck and helps with loading and unloading. It is a union requirement that teamsters be hired anytime a vehicle is used in a commercial shoot, whether it is on camera as part of the commercial or for transporting personnel or equipment.

Telephoto Lens A long-focus lens that enables a cameraman to take close-up shots of a subject from relatively far distances.

Test Market A portion of the country set aside to test a new product or a new advertising campaign for an existing product. Depending on the scope of the test, a test market can be as small as one city or as large as several states.

Test Market Commercial   A commercial shot for use only in a test market.

Three-Dimensional   An illusion of depth.

Tied-Off   Expression used to describe a shot from a locked-down camera position.

Tight Shot   Any close shot.

Tilt   The swiveling of the camera in a vertical arc.

Tracking   *See* Dollying

Traffic Department   The department in an advertising agency responsible for seeing that prints of commercials get to the right television stations at the right time.

Treble   The upper half of the musical-pitch range.

Trim Barrel   A barrel that looks much like a large garbage can lined with a cloth bag. Attached to its top is a metal frame with wire pegs. The trim barrel is used to hold pieces of film and sound track trimmed from a commercial.

Trims   Pieces of film cut from scenes being edited into a rough cut.

Tripod   A three-legged support for the camera.

Trucking   Moving the camera laterally while it is shooting. *See also* Dollying.

Twenty-Eight and a Half Seconds   The exact amount of time available for the sound track in a thirty-second commercial.

Twenty-Four Frames per Second   Standard speed of film as it runs through a projector.

Two-Shot   A shot that includes two people.

Umbrella   A umbrella-shaped lighting accessory whose reflective surface is intended to provide "bounce" illumination.

Undercrank   To run the camera at a slower speed than normal. This gives the illusion of speeded-up action when the film is projected at normal speed.

Underexpose   To fail to allow enough light to reach the film.

Up Shot   Shot made from a low position with the camera angled up.

Upstage   Portion of the set farthest from the camera.

Videotape   Material used to record both sound and picture for electronic photography. It varies in width from one-half to two inches.

The tape's sensitive surface consists of a layer of iron oxide particles approximately one-sixth the thickness of a human hair.

Vignette 1. A commercial featuring several short scenes involving different actors or situations, all of which make the same point. 2. A picture that does not fill the entire screen; the edges of the frame are blurred while the center remains in focus.

Visual Special Effects Opticals.

Voice-Over (V.O.) Announcer lines recorded after the commercial is edited. These lines are placed in scenes shot without sound and usually describe what the viewer is seeing.

Walk-Through A casual rehearsal to familiarize the actors with their blocking.

Wardrobe The clothing worn by the talent in commercials.

Wardrobe Attendant Crew member; keeps clothing pressed and repaired during the shooting day.

Warm Word used to describe a reddish or yellowish film print.

Washout An overexposure of the film resulting in loss of the image.

Whip (Snap Pan) A quick pan of the camera from one area to another.

Wide-Angle Lens Any lens with a short focal length that has an angle of coverage of 45 degrees or more.

Wide Shot A shot that encompasses a whole scene.

Wild Track A sound track recorded without the camera running.

Wild Wall A wall that can be rather easily moved from one part of the set to another during the shooting day.

Wing To shoot a scene without rehearsal.

Wipe An optical effect; one scene is brought into another by moving a line across the frame.

Work Print A print from the original footage used to edit the commercial. The rough cut is created from the work print.

Wrap The end of the shoot.

Writer Member of the agency creative team who writes the copy for advertising.

Zoom To use a special lens for going from a long shot to a close-up or vice versa without moving the camera.

Zoom Lens Lens used for going from a long shot to a close-up without moving the camera.